About the Author

Anne Marie Scanlon was born in Ireland and has lived in New York for ten years. After various careers as a P.R. executive, stand-up comic, commodities trader and executive director of the non-profit Emerald Isle Immigration Center, she began writing. In the past two years, Anne Marie has contributed columns to a number of newspapers on both sides of the Atlantic, including the weekly *New York Doll* for the *Evening Herald*. She has also worked as a broadcast journalist with RTÉ Radio and writes regularly about beauty and fashion and is never happier than when she is purchasing a new handbag.

It's not Me . . . it's You!

A girl's guide to dating in Ireland

Anne Marie Scanlon

POOLBEG

Published 2005
by Poolbeg Press Ltd
123 Grange Hill, Baldoyle
Dublin 13, Ireland
E-mail: poolbeg@poolbeg.com
www.poolbeg.com

1 3 5 7 9 10 8 6 4 2

A catalogue record for this book is available from the British Library.

ISBN 1 84223 250 9

Foreword © Marian Keyes
Illustrations © Zink Design
Author photograph © Nicola McClean

Typeset by Patricia Hope in Bembo 11/13.75
Printed by Litografia Rosés, S.A, Spain

www.poolbeg.com

Acknowledgements

Despite the name on the cover this book has been a collaborative effort and I owe a debt of gratitude to many many people. First, to my Mum, Nora Scanlon — for everything. I love you loads.

To Marian Keyes and Tony Baines for their unending support, kindness, patience and generosity. Words cannot express how much I owe to both of you, God knows what I did to deserve such wonderful friends. You are karma in action. Special thanks to Marian for letting me borrow the expression Betty Bothways.

To Caitriona Keyes and Paula Rice, two of the best friends a girl could ask for, there's nothing toxic about either of you. To Eamonn Dornan, Tracey Ferguson, Joseph McCarron, Ib Soliman and Fiona Walsh for all of the craic and making New York feel like home.

To the Loreto Girls for always believing in me, Nicola Byrne, Fiona McHugh, Kyla O'Kelly, Keelin Shanley and especially Deborah Pearce who provided me with advice, encouragement and lovely dinners. To Martina Devlin, a wonderful writer and great friend. To Freda & Kappa Grealy,

Vicky McCabe & Gary Pillow, Siobhan & Mick O'Hara, Isabel Ryan & John O'Connell and Kevin & Natalie Perry for their hospitality over the years. To Christina Kirshbaum & Turlough McConnell for all the fun and the stories.

To all the girls who shared their stories with me especially Suzeanne Benson, Denise DeCurtis, Rosaleen Doherty, Danielle Koza, Suki Kuss, Lorraine Murphy, Carolyn Ryan-Murin and Joanne O'Connell. To the late and very lovely Jack Holland for giving me a start. To Paula Campbell, Emma Walsh, Claire McVeigh and my editor Anne O'Sullivan at Poolbeg. To David Lawlor, Frank Coughlin and everyone at the *Evening Herald*. To Paddy McCarthy, Tony Quinn and everyone at *Irish Connections*. To Nicola McClean for the lovely photos. To Gabrielle Vitellio for legal, and Ed Keough for financial advice. To the boys in The Green Room for listening. To Jim Allison and Kevin Barry for you know what. To Mark Byrne for the good times.

Finally to all the boys I've gone out with over the years, even the lousers. Without you there would be no book.

Foreword

by Marian Keyes

A riddle, wrapped around a mystery, cloaked in a dirty Leitrim jersey – *that* is a man. Give me the third secret of Fatima, the Enigma Code, or Advanced Su Doku any day of the week – men are far, far harder to fathom.

But not to worry. Anne Marie will sort you out. Everything, yes everything, you need to know about those strange impenetrable creatures called men is contained within. Where to find them. How to entrance them. What they *really* mean when they say, "I'll call you tomorrow at 9 pm on the dot, so help me God, on my granny's grave."

It's all here. Instructions on how to successfully speed date, how to handle his mammy, how to break it off with him (say, 'It's not me, it's you,' of course) and how to get over a break-up (get fluthered every night for a month and savour the break-up-induced weight-loss.)

And I'd just like to sort out a little confusion here – there's no shame in wanting a boyfriend. You can be a good feminist and still like men. *Nice* men, that is. Men who treat you with respect. There's no point in having a boyfriend just for the sake of it, because God only knows what sort of oddballs you'd end up with. You're better off with none at all in that case.

It's not Me, it's You is an absolute hoot and an invaluable textbook for those looking for a fella, or those saddled with one they want to get rid of or even those lucky devils who are happily in love. I hope you enjoy it as much as I did.

Contents

A Field Guide To The Irish Male

Introduction

Why? Who? Where? When? How?

Why buy this book? Well, let me let you in on a little secret. The boys of Ireland don't want you to. Why? Because dating, as opposed to going out with someone, places the balance of power firmly with *you*. That's why. Apart from that, a lot of boys don't understand how to date. It's like the old joke:

Q: What is an Irish boy's idea of a good date?
A: "I'll get the first round, you find some seats."

Of course, they don't want you to read this book.

What, you wonder, gives me the right to write a dating guide? Fair question. That one, you might well be saying to yourself, what does she know about men. Is she even married? Well, no, I'm not married and hence I know quite a lot about being *Out There*. I've put *years* of dedicated research into this book just for you! And if that wasn't enough to be going on

1

with, I've also included a *Field Guide To The Irish Male,* a quick manual to help you sort out the boys from the boys.

As I come from Ireland, the whole concept of dating was initially very hard for me to grasp. When I first went to New York I resisted the whole notion of formal dates, as they were far too alien a concept. Instead, I persisted in the traditional Irish manner i.e. getting plastered and snogging someone. Eventually out of necessity (I stopped drinking) I was forced to embrace the notion of 'dating'. It was either that or face a life of celibacy. Not that hard a decision in the end. And, one of the best things that ever happened to me, which is why I'm going to tell you all about it.

The first thing you need for a date is someone to go with. The single biggest complaint I hear from girls is that they just can't meet fellas. Well, read on. I'll tell you WHERE, WHEN *and* HOW. The WHO is up to you but I'll give you a few pointers on the best way to spot Mr. Right (or even Mr. Right Now).

Part One

Is There Anyone Out There?

Who is the right boy for you?

Is There Anyone Out There?

Chapter One

Mr. Right or Mr Right Now?

What kind of boy are you looking for?

You decide

So you want to meet a fella with the view to forming a relationship. This is the book for you. First though, like a job, a car or an outfit, you have to decide what you want. A man, you say. No eejits need apply. Fair enough.

Before you rush ahead to Part Two *(Location, Location, Location)*, let's just pause for a moment to take a look at the elements that make a successful pairing.

1. Physical Attraction.
2. Shared Interests and Goals.

OK, babe, we'll leave the physical attraction part aside for a second and take a look at shared interests and goals. If you're dying to have children then obviously you are not going to be happy with a fella who is allergic to the sight of nappies. LISTEN when he says he comes out in a rash when he's anywhere near a toddler. Why would he lie?

Beauty-and-the-Beast Complex

This is a mistake girls make time and time again. I can change him. NO, YOU CAN'T. Really you can't. The same goes for a man who says he's not interested in commitment. Please, please, please believe him. Save yourself and your poor long-suffering girlfriends from all of the anguish and agony that will follow if you pursue this man. Leave him alone.

Face it; if the house was burning down around you, you wouldn't for a second think that you could talk the fire into stopping. If you broke your ankle in a roller-skating accident, you'd go to casualty, not try to *think* yourself back to health. The same goes for relationships. If a man is up-front enough to be honest about his needs you should be thrilled. There are enough lousers out there who will lie through their teeth, so an honest man is a thing to be treasured. Or not, as the case may be. If your needs and his are different, then go your own way and let him go his.

Know your own mind

If you know what you want before you head *Out There*, then you have more chance of finding it. More important than knowing what you want, know what you *don't* want.

What are the things that are absolute no-nos?

1.
2.
3.
4.
5.

It's all relative but for the record I consider the following gentlemen to be out of bounds:

Married Men

Apart from the morality issue, taking up with a married man, or with a gentleman who cohabits with his partner, is not a good idea. Relationships between two people are hard enough at the best of times; when you triangulate them, fuggetaboutit.

It is nearly impossible to have a normal relationship with a married guy. You cannot go on holidays together, go to the cinema on the spur of the moment, go out for meals without looking over your shoulder or lounge around the house reading the Sunday papers. You have to adhere to his schedule and be on-call for whenever he gets a minute away from his wife and/or family. You are permanently on-hold and this is not being fair to yourself.

Some married guys do leave their wives for their girlfriends but they are very few and far between. Even then, it's not always a hand-in-hand-into-the-sunset scenario. The transition from a clandestine relationship to the mundane repetition of everyday life can be difficult if not impossible. And don't forget about that constant niggling suspicion you'll have to live with – the little voice in your head saying 'If he did it to her, he could do it to me too'.

Grainne got involved with a married man who was 'separated' from his wife. What he neglected to tell her was that the separation was a temporary one to give them both breathing space. Unfortunately Grainne didn't realise that his marriage wasn't over until after she had found out she was pregnant. What she didn't know was that another woman (not his wife) was also pregnant. What a prince!

Saoirse's story is quite different. She was in her teens when she became involved with Shay, a friend of her older brother whom she'd known for most of her life. "I'd been mad about him since I was twelve," she said. After six months Shay left his wife for Saoirse and they were together for eleven years. "I wanted to get married but he had a bit of an issue with commitment," Saoirse recalled. "One time I thought I might be pregnant and he said if I was that he'd marry me. I was furious. If we got married I wanted him to marry me because of who I am, not because I was having a baby."

Serial Killers

OK, I'll admit it's sometimes hard to figure out who these guys are until after the fact.

Inmates of the 'Joy or a Similar Institution

Yes, I know that seems like an obvious one but you'd be surprised at the number of women who start relationships with convicted felons. I don't get it. Surely, part of the reason you want a boyfriend is to have someone to go to Sunday brunch with and to bring you Lemsip when you are sick. If they're incarcerated in the Big House they're pretty useless in that regard, just like married men in fact.

Other Gentlemen with Criminal Records

Oh, come on, these lads are only glamorous in *The Sopranos*. In reality they are a sad lot.

Actors

Q: What do you call an actor without a girlfriend?
A: Homeless

Actors are terrible boyfriends. They hog the bathroom and they badger you incessantly for positive reinforcement. How was I? Was I good? Did you like it? What was your favourite part? "I'm the best at this amn't I? None of your other boyfriends were a patch on me, were they?" These are questions that actors can and WILL apply to any activity they undertake, be it playing a part, cooking, sex – it's endless. God forbid you answer them with anything other than "Brilliant", "Excellent", "It was the best", "Absolutely. You have ruined me for other men."

Even writing that down exhausted me. Now think how tiring it would be to keep up the endless ego-bolstering day after day, night after night. Then there's the drama. Actors don't like to keep their 'craft' (puke) on stage; they like to bring it home with them and most of them would give the average two-year-old a good run for his money in the tantrum throwing stakes. Who needs the stress? Furthermore they are constantly broke and forever flirting with their co-stars.

Musicians *See Actors.*

Tell me what you want, what you really really want.

Now what do you want? What is *essential* for a future long-term boyfriend?

1

2

3

4

5

A steady income would definitely be on my list. I've been coupled with too many tortured artists (i.e. penniless writers/artists/actors/musicians) in the past. I'd also want someone who was trustworthy and reliable, a man who when he says he's going to do something will actually follow through and do it. This is something that applies across the board from doing the washing up to getting up at the crack of dawn to drive me to the airport. I've been in relationships with men who promised the world but couldn't do something as simple as buy stamps. Promises are cheap. Keep an eye out as actions really do speak louder than words.

If you know what you want, and more importantly what you *don't* want, Mr. Right will be easier to find. Paradoxically, don't overburden yourself with a checklist and price yourself out of the market entirely. If you are unrealistically specific and want to date only a man who is between the ages of 30-37, between 5' 10" and 6' 1" with blond hair, blue eyes, never been married, no children from previous relationships, with a sizeable monetary and physical endowment, then good luck with that one.

Try to keep an open mind when you meet a man. Don't write him off immediately because you don't fall on your knees panting with lust at the very first glance. Some men will knock you sideways initially, and often three months later you come out of your lust-induced daze and ask, 'What the hell am I doing with this fool?' Other guys are slow burners; the more you get to know them the more you like them. So keep that in mind.

Flexibility Doesn't Mean Bending Over Backwards

So you've made your two lists. What you definitely want and

what you definitely don't want. So you're clear what's a big no–no and what's a go–go–go.

Like everything else there has to be some middle ground, some areas where you can compromise. Obviously if you are a devout Catholic and a member of the Legion of Mary, then religion might not be the area where you are willing to compromise. And that's OK. This isn't a lesson in political correctness. If your religion is important to you and you don't want to go out with someone from a different religious background, that's fine. It's your choice.

What about tidiness? If you are compulsively tidy (guilty) would you be able to reach a compromise with a complete slob or would you find yourself in court charged with Grievous Bodily Harm? Is there a middle ground between a fella who thinks dining out is going to Abrakebabra and a girl who thinks a restaurant is a place with a dress code other than 'No shirt. No shoes. No Service.'? Only you can decide where exactly you draw the line between acceptable and unacceptable.

You may as well figure out the areas that are open to compromise now. If you want to have a *Significant Other* (S.O.) in your life, finding the middle ground is something you'll need to become very familiar with.

In the case of what type of potential BF you'd like, we'll call the compromise position the *Maybes*. For example, you're looking for a man with a job, no ifs, ands or buts; he MUST be employed. That's non–negotiable. So what's negotiable? Plenty. You might not be all that picky about what sort of job he has, just that he has one. Maybe you want a man who's a highly driven ambitious workaholic or perhaps you would prefer someone who has a more laid-back attitude. You may not care that he's not a multi-millionaire just that he's solvent. You don't mind that he has kids from a previous relationship just as long as he fulfils his parental obligations to them.

Say you meet a boy and he's fanatical about Celtic/ Arsenal/Man United. You haven't a clue; you don't know the offside rule from a hole in the wall and have never understood a bunch of grown men running around a freezing cold pitch in the middle of winter. However, your new beau has a season ticket and that means that every Saturday from here to next year is booked out. What do you do? This is where you get flexible my friend. What you don't do is say, "Now look Johnnie, we're a couple now and as such I expect you to spend your weekends with me." That is a one-way ticket back to singleville.

Yes, it would be nice to have your BF around at the weekends but it's not essential to a healthy relationship. Football is his *thing*. If he asks you to go to a game with him, then go. He's inviting you to share something that's important to him, that he loves. Go, make the sacrifice, do it for him. On the other hand, if he demands that you accompany him to every single game, home and away, and "you'll bloody well enjoy it", then that's his express ticket back to Losertown, or it SHOULD be.

The new BF might be very actively involved in playing a particular sport and want you to take it up. Give it a go. Seriously, at least try. You never know you might discover a passion that will outlast the relationship and give you far more pleasure in the long run. If a boy wants you to take up squash or golf or paintballing, he's inviting you to do something that's important to him. Show willing. If you turn out to be crap at whatever activity he's so mad about, then no harm done — at least you both tried.

> *Theresa always sneered at anything that even hinted of sci-fi yet somehow ended up married to a man who was addicted to* Star Trek. *Just to be clear here, he liked watching it on the telly; he didn't get dressed up as Mr. Spock and head off to dodgy Trekker conventions in even dodgier hotels. Theresa started watching the programme with him as a gesture, even though she thought the whole thing was a load of wank. Guess who now has every* Star Wars *and* Lord of the Rings *DVD?*

Politics can be a maybe too. As long as both sides agree to respect the other's political views then casting different votes at election time need not be an impediment to a successful relationship. Well, in theory at least. It wouldn't work for me, but it all depends just how passionate you are in your political beliefs.

Finally when making your lists of what you *Want/Don't Want* try to remember the difference between what you'd like and what is essential. What you would *like* should go on the negotiable list; what is essential will be covered by your *Want/Don't Want* lists.

All The Good Ones Are Taken

So we're agreed you cannot change a man. Right. Don't despair, however; although you cannot change him, there are some *things about him* you can change. Trivial things, like hair and clothes. Never ever discount a man on the basis of his shoes. Almost every boyfriend I have had has been the proud owner of dodgy footwear. Now obviously some of these men were as dodgy as their worn-out penny loafers (do you realise how much it hurts to admit that I went out with someone who wore penny loafers?), as cheap as their knackered runners and as naff as the Jesus sandals they wore with socks.

(Actually I've never gone out with a man who wore Jesus sandals, either with or without socks. Come on, a girl has to draw the line somewhere.) On the other hand, plenty of the men with the crap footwear were lovely fellas and great boyfriends and I would have missed out if I'd turned them down simply because they appeared to have very bad taste in shoes.

You know how it seems as though all the good ones are taken? Pity you can't see pictures of them *before* they started going out with their present wives/girlfriends.

> *I lived with Sean for two years. When I first met him he had a dodgy haircut and an even dodgier wardrobe. You should have seen him by the time we broke up. He was stunning. Honestly, he couldn't walk down the street without women doing double-takes At the end of the relationship I felt a bit cheated, like I'd put money in the bank and some other woman was going to benefit from the principal and the interest. However, as my friend Emma pointed out to me, how many times have I been the beneficiary of some other woman's hard work? As the old saying goes, what goes around comes around.*

Moulding Not Mouldy

This process of transforming a man from drippy to dapper is called 'moulding' and is not half as sinister as it sounds. Most straight men invariably look to their wives and girlfriends for sartorial advice anyway, so it's not all that tough. Sometimes it occurs the other way round, but this happens about as often as Halley's Comet.

I have seen several men transformed by their wives and LTG's (long-term girlfriends). Like most things, moulding isn't something which takes place overnight; it's a process which takes time. You can't expect your man to adopt a whole new wardrobe and hairstyle instantaneously. He won't. Unless you surprise him with five homosexuals and a TV crew, but what are the chances of that? No, you need to introduce items of clothing gradually. Very graaaaaddddualllly. Get him a nice shirt for his birthday; offer to go with him when he goes shopping.

Mossy started married life with a scruffy beard and a fondness for old jumpers but has since undergone a complete sartorial transformation at the hands of his wife. "I was a bit dubious at first," Mossy told me. "But bedad, the gay lads have started checking me out in the gym and you know you're looking good when the gay lads start giving you the eye."

A Field Guide to the Irish Male

Patriotic Paddy

How to Spot Him:

The Patriot would give his life in the cause of Irish freedom and the liberation of the six counties, as long as it doesn't involve him having to get out of his chair or learn Irish. He has the 'cupla focal' which he scatters throughout his conversation and he feels that is sufficient. His conversation is also liberally scattered with the terms 'British Imperialism' and 'Good Friday Agreement'. The Patriot is often seen wearing a moss-green Aran sweater. He bought it in British Home Stores but cut the label off and tells people it was knitted in Armagh Women's Prison. He could do with a haircut but who has time to make an appointment when they're busy struggling against 'the Brits'? His dirty little secret is that he actually supports Man United.

Habitat:

Anywhere *An Phoblacht* is sold; political rallies and protest marches.

What he says:

"*Tiochfaidh Ár Lá*" "Our boys . . ."

What you'll never hear him say:

"Thatcher wasn't a bad ould burd."

Chapter Two

Love, Lust or a Bout of Flu?

What do sweaty palms and butterflies in the tummy really mean?

Love at first sight?

Why do we fancy certain people and not others? Let me count the ways:

1. Physical appearance
2. Similarity
3. Proximity

Yes, proximity. How can you fancy someone if he's not in your immediate sphere? There could be a gorgeous, perfectly wonderful dude wandering around downtown Reykjavic at this very moment but you'll never fancy him, unless he hops on a plane and just happens to be browsing in your local Spar at the exact same moment that you are there purchasing a packet of Cream Crackers and a litre of milk.

Let's forget about the Icelandic Lust King for now. Obviously physical nearness is a factor in fancying someone. However, continued exposure (increased proximity) improves your chances of falling for someone and vice versa. How often have you heard a girl say, "I didn't fancy him at first. He just sort of grew on me."? The more familiar a person becomes to you the more likely you are to like him, and to relax in his company.

Let's Get Physical

Thank God that not everyone finds the same things attractive. I'd take Dara O'Briain over Brad Pitt any day. Seriously. I think Mr. O'Briain is extremely smart and very funny. Apart from that, I've always had a bit of a thing about baldies. Now having said that there are some universal standards. A woman with a third eye in the middle of her forehead is rather unlikely to win the Miss World competition – not on this world anyway. And although some gentlemen can turn a blind eye to unwashed hair and gravy-stained leggings, most won't.

It is a truth universally acknowledged that the more confident someone is in themselves, the sexier they appear to others. Honestly, sexiness isn't about dress size, boob measurement or possessing a shapely ankle – it's about being comfortable in your own skin. That's what translates to the rest of the world and the opposite sex.

Two Of A Kind

Forget the romantic novels and the *Jerry Springer* specials (mousey librarian marries freak with all-over body tattoo and teeth filed into points). People who are very different from each other are unlikely to form a bond. On occasion continued exposure (proximity) to someone you dislike will lead to your actually liking him. The majority of the time, though, everything he does and says will confirm your initial opinion and what began as a mild dislike can end up as not being able to stand the sight of him.

Generally people go for other people similar to themselves because:

A. Nobody likes being contradicted. If you believe in a woman's right to choose and you hook up with a man who spends his weekends marching in pro-life parades, how long do you give it? It doesn't even have to be that dramatic. Most people do not like being disagreed with. If you find someone who shares your opinions and world view, this validates you and boosts self-esteem. It will also make for a more harmonious life.

B. Very simply, we think that people who think like us will like us. It goes without saying this is often the case: if it wasn't the world wouldn't have as many clubs and associations as it does. Only one trainspotter can truly value another trainspotter.

Is this love that I'm feeling?

So do all of these things add up to love? Maybe? They most definitely describe lust.

Lust at first sight should not be confused with love.

Lust is a drug. Physical attraction triggers hormones and chemicals that have an intoxicating effect on the body and mind. Oh yes, pheromones. The biological definition of pheromones, "a chemical substance excreted by an animal which triggers reproductive behaviour response from a recipient of the same species," dates back to 1959. Translation – chemicals manufactured by your body that make people fancy you. In some cases the pheromones will have a far more powerful effect than your appearance, (which explains a lot about the men who turn a blind eye to greasy hair and gravy stains).

Perfect Scents

Humans detect pheromones subliminally via scent. That's why it's often a good idea to go easy on the perfume, as you could be masking the natural scent which would have fellas baying and pawing at your front door. Not everyone responds in kind to individual scents. What could leave your best friend whimpering with lust might leave you completely cold. A recent survey by the Monell Chemical Senses Center in Philadelphia found that not only do individuals respond differently to various natural scents but that gay men and lesbian women prefer different scents from their heterosexual counterparts, which makes perfect sense when you think about it.

Sinead was the third woman Zac asked out. He was very specific about how to screen out future girlfriends. First, helping a girl to take off her coat provided the opportunity to get a good whiff of her. Girl number one "didn't smell right". It wasn't B.O; she was just lacking that certain something. Although girl number two "smelled really good," her bad table manners – speaking with her mouth full, marked her card for her. Girl number three, my friend Sinead, passed the smell test and knew how to conduct a conversation without spraying Zac and the table with half masticated food. They've been married for over ten years now. So don't discount your natural smell – or indeed your table manners.

THE FULL MONTY

Lust is often confused with love as it produces the same physical reactions: butterflies in the tummy, distraction, a feeling of wellbeing, loss of appetite and an inability to sleep. For a LTR (long-term relationship) to work you need a little bit more than fizzing popping chemicals, delightful though they are. You need:

A. Shared Goals
B. Common Interests

I once shacked up with a man who I had nothing in common with. We were deliriously in lust and in our mutual madness decided to cohabit. Everyone knows that nothing tarnishes the sheen of chemical co-dependency more quickly than the mundane business of everyday life: bills, grocery shopping, bills, house-cleaning, bills, the toilet seat being up, bills, his dodgy friends, bills, your friends that he doesn't like and did I mention bills? Money, and its lack of elasticity, is the biggest stressor on most live-in relationships and ours was no different.

Apart from our cash issues there were other problems that plagued the relationship from the get-go, ones that we would have seen coming if saner minds had prevailed. For example, I read compulsively. I get nervous if I find myself without something to read. More than nervous. I can't get on a plane without a book. I read in bed, on the bus, and once attempted it on the treadmill at the gym with horrifically embarrassing results. I subscribe to so many publications that the postman HATES me. Books, magazines, and newspapers are an integral, essential part of my life. In the two years that this gentleman and I kept house together he read a total of two books. Two books in two years! I read two books in a week.

Now OK, I'll admit that a relationship between a non-reader and a compulsive reader is feasible, but only if they have some other common ground. We didn't. Sexual relations and partying were the glue that held that relationship together. Sexual relations and partying don't make strong glue – believe me. For me, being with this man was as insane as a devout capitalist settling down with a diehard socialist. In other words it was doomed before it even began.

But that's not going to happen to you, is it? Not at all. You've made your lists and you know the difference between a virus that will pass in a couple of days and true love. So you have a pretty firm idea of the type WHO you'd like to meet; let's take a look at WHERE.

A Field Guide to the Irish Male

The Crim

How to Spot Him:

The Crim likes to portray himself as the biggest thing to hit the underworld since The General. He talks a lot about 'jobs' and 'heists' and operates on a need-to-know basis. The Crim likes gold bracelets and rings and never pays for anything with less than a twenty-euro note. In reality the closest he's come to a bank job was fiddling his Nan's change when he did her messages (last week).

Habitat:

Flashing his wads in nightclubs at night. Hanging around pool halls during the day.

What he says:

"I need to see a man about a dog, yerknowwhaImean." He taps the side of his nose and winks a lot.

What you'll never hear him say:

"Somebody call the guards."

25

Part Two

Location, Location, Location

Boys are a bit like houses; you have
to look in the right places

Let the games begin

Chapter Three

Boys love sport

Let the games begin

There, I could have just written that one sentence and left it at that. Wherever sports are played you will find the male of the species, either taking part or moaning from the sidelines about how much better he woulda, coulda done it.

Playing Footie

Football is the obvious choice. Now, before you rush out and buy a season ticket for the nearest football club, be warned. Football is like a religion for most men. You'd hardly try to get off with a fella in the middle of Mass; well, at least I hope you wouldn't. Think on. When they're at the football stadium they're there to watch the game. You could prance half-naked across the pitch and the only response you'll get from the menfolk in the stalls is 'Get off'. Not you'll notice, 'Get 'em off'.

Having said that, taking an active interest in football and

getting involved with a club will bring you into contact with plenty of guys who will be well impressed with your enthusiasm for, and knowledge of, their beloved game.

Getting Teed Off

I can never understand the male obsession with golf. How can guys be so enamoured of a game where they try to get a relatively large ball into a relatively small hole when the same lads find it next to impossible to get a thin stream of urine into the gaping yawning chasm of the toilet?

OK, all questions aside, guys appear to give the same amount of time, energy and love to golf that we girls devote to shoes. More even. Unlike footie you can easily take up golf as a pastime. If you are like me and have the hand-to-eye coordination of a cross-eyed drunk, do not despair. You don't have to actually play golf to hang out at golf courses. All of the action takes place in the 19th hole (the pub to the rest of us) anyway.

A Load of Balls

Anyone for tennis? Kill two birds with one racket. Tennis clubs and tournaments are a great way of expanding your social network and keeping in shape. Plus if a guy looks good in his tennis rig-out you can rest assured he's going to look good in anything, or indeed in nothing. The same can be said for fellas in basketball shorts. If you want to get involved in basketball either play the game or support it. Do not attempt to become a cheerleader. Why? It will damage your chances of ever being taken seriously again in your entire life and besides everyone despises cheerleaders. All right, maybe not everyone, but I do and it's my book, so there you go.

Good Rides

Steady, I'll get to that later. The Irish are famous for a number of things and one of them is horses. We love horses, breeding them, racing them, betting on them – there's no end to the craic we can get out of a good ride. There are equestrian centres and pony clubs the length and breadth of the country so if you fancy a canter there's little excuse.

I'm personally opposed to fox-hunting and for like-minded people there are drag-hunts which are a great way of meeting a wide variety of people. These are usually followed by a Hunt Ball, which is just a fancy way of saying piss-up.

Tag Rugby

Don't let the name put you off. It's not really a sport. However, it is the hottest way of meeting fellas around right now. Instead of physically tackling members of the opposing team you quite literally tear strips off them. All right, never mind how it actually works. Sign up for a team as soon as you can as places are like gold dust. Apart from the game itself there are all kinds of activities attached to the leagues – barbeques, dinners and hitting the pub to cool down after.

Jenny went to a Tag Rugby party dolled up to the nines because she fancied one of the players. When he did eventually put in an appearance it was only to leave less than ten minutes later. Jenny wasn't too upset as in the meantime she'd been busy chatting to another gorgeous fella who she's been going out with ever since.

31

Swap the rubber gloves . . .

For a pair of boxing gloves. Seriously, boxing is one of the best ways of keeping in shape and apart from the sport being full of men there's always a chance you'll pick up some neat self-defence moves. If boxing isn't to your taste there are plenty of different martial arts classes around where you can

A. Keep in shape.
B. Learn to defend yourself.
C. Meet guys.

Cupid's Arrow

If you're a competitive sort of lassie then Archery and Fencing are two sports where you can indulge your competitive nature while learning new skills and meeting new people.

Play Your Cards Right

If your idea of hell is pointed implements, coming down the side of a mountain on a bit of wood or having to spend more than five minutes in the outdoors, don't worry. There's always bridge. Now, I can't personally attest to the pulling quotient at the average Bridge Club because I haven't the slightest clue how to play. However I have heard of people meeting their fellas at bridge and other card games.

Don't forget Poker which is the sexy card game of the moment.

A Field Guide to the Irish Male

Sport Billy

How to Spot Him:

When he's not out kicking a ball, lobbing a ball across a net, or putting a ball across a green, he's wearing a soccer strip, a baseball hat supporting a rugby team and carrying a sports bag with the name of an American basketball team on it.

Habitat:

Football stadia, on aeroplanes with hundreds of other Sport Billys en route to away games, in front of the telly screaming at the screen.

What he says:

"Yeeeessssss!!!!" "Gooooooaaaaaalllll!"

What you'll never hear him say:

"It's only a game."

Chapter Four

Out to Sea

It's a shore thing

Getting Wet

Boys just love the water. Boats, yachts, diving, swimming, fishing, canoeing, water skiing. I hesitate to use the term 'water sports' because it is also a term for a particular (a very particular) sexual activity. Any pastime that takes place on or in water, on or around boats and similar vessels will always have a heavy testosterone quotient.

"But I don't know how to splice a mainbrace or which way is port," you wail. Easily fixed. Go to a class. There are plenty of classes out there. Deep-sea diving or scuba-diving holidays are a great way for pasty-skinned Celtic girls to meet boys. Most packages have activities for people with varied degrees of skill, from beginner on up. Lying around on a beach for two weeks is fine but wouldn't you like a change?

Working vacations and adventure holidays are increasing in

popularity. For example, you can sign on to become a crew member on a yacht or similar vessel. This is a great way not only of meeting boys, but of getting some exercise and completely expanding your horizons.

If you don't fancy getting your hair wet then there are plenty of other activity holidays that are perfect for people holidaying in groups or by themselves. Whatever your own interests there are plenty of packages available for example cycling holidays which are brilliant for people on their own. If you're a bit like me and don't fancy that degree of exertion, there are always walking holidays.

Share and Share Alike

In New York one of the ways people combine leisure and meeting new people is to take a summer share in places like the Hamptons and Cape Cod. NY becomes so hot and humid during the summer months that it's practically intolerable, so it's nice to be able to escape to the beach at the weekend. Unless you are Bill Gates, the high rental price of summer homes means the only way to cover the cost is to share the property with as many individuals as possible. Not everyone has 26 or more friends that they can share the expense with, so renting with a bunch of strangers is the norm.

I know this isn't really an option for Irish people as we don't really have a very reliable summer. But the same principle applies to other weekend activities centred on or around the water. Ireland has the longest network of inland waterways purely for pleasure-cruising in Europe. What could be easier than putting together a group of people to take to the water for the weekend? Apart from the chances of meeting someone whom you didn't know before onboard, there's the craic when you dock and meet the people from the other craft.

If inland waterways aren't exciting enough for you, there are more than enough sailing clubs in Ireland. For those who like to get a little bit closer to the water Ireland has many canoeing and kayaking organisations which operate year round. Apart from boating, in its many guises, this little island of ours can offer Sub-aqua Diving, Waterskiing, Windsurfing and Surfing. Forget Hawaii, Ireland is now one of *the* destinations for serious surfers and what girl doesn't like a surfer?

Snow Business

Even though the summer doesn't afford Irish people great opportunities for communal living and bonding, don't despair. Skiing holidays and ski houses provide plenty of opportunities to meet and mingle with a whole bunch of new people. As with other activities holiday packages are available for every level of expertise. Winter sports aren't confined to skiing; there's snowboarding and even snowshoeing (winter walking).

A Field Guide to the Irish Male

The Fisherman

How to Spot Him:

The Fisherman likes to make himself inconspicuously conspicuous. He's part-martyr, part-braggart. He is constantly putting himself down but not in a genuine way. His comments aren't genuine just a way of getting you to contradict him and tell him how utterly wonderful he is. He will say that he's really ugly which is your prompt to say, "Oh no, Jamie, you are so NOT ugly. Why you are beyond handsome, a perfect specimen of manhood if ever there was one." He'll loudly diss his golf game which is your cue to say, "For shame, Seamus, nobody and I mean, nobody could outdo you at golf. I bet if you ever played Tiger Woods you'd thrash him." If you don't make the appropriate response to his perpetual self-denigration he will sulk up a storm.

Habitat:

On the golf course, in the kitchen, at the local karaoke bar, anywhere he has an audience.

What he says:

"Oh God no, I'm lousy at that, the worst" accompanied by a deprecating smile.

What you'll never hear him say:

"I'm pretty pleased with myself."

Chapter Five

Meanwhile Back on Dry Land

Plenty of places to find fellas

Many girls hate sport in all its shapes and forms. That doesn't mean that you can't meet boys. There are plenty of other places for those of us whose idea of exercise is striking a match to light up.

Charity Begins At Home

Voluntary work is not only a wonderful way of expanding your social circles and horizons but it's also a great way to boost flagging self-esteem. There are more than enough organisations that need your help – soup kitchens, homeless shelters, literacy programmes; the list is a long one. Some programmes will be more fitted to your purpose than others.

Self Self Self

Now I just know that someone is going to tackle me about this and say that suggesting voluntary work as a way of meeting fellas cheapens the self-sacrifice of 'genuine' volunteers. A word to the person who's thinking of saying that to me – don't. You won't like the answer. Nobody, I repeat NOBODY, does anything without a personal agenda. I worked for many years in the non-profit sector and I know what motivates people to volunteer their time. Make no mistake about this, everyone has some sort of ulterior motive. Certainly there are very good people out there who give generously of their time to help others. Some of them are burning advocates of the 'cause' – the mission of the charity; some are networking for business or personal gain; some are just plain bored or lonely. If you do some good in the course of looking for a relationship, that doesn't make you a bad person or any less valuable a volunteer than the person whose motives are 'pure'.

Now having said that let me add if you are volunteering solely to meet men then don't. Your primary aim should be the work that the organisation is doing. You have your own reasons also – and those are:

1. Getting out and about
2. Meeting new people

When you're doing both, the chances of meeting a nice fella rise exponentially.

Choose an organisation that you feel some passion or commitment towards otherwise you will not enjoy the experience, nor will those who are unfortunate enough to have to work with you.

You can combine charity work and an adventure holiday by volunteering for a charity-trek or expedition.

Liz met her fella on a charity walk in Vietnam. "I didn't know anyone else on the trip," she said. "I missed the orientation day when everyone meets up, because I got a place at the last minute due to a cancellation." However, Liz was only one of many who were on the trip by themselves and found it wasn't hard to get to know people. She met Philip on the first day in Hanoi, although he later told her that he'd spotted her at the airport. "Somehow we always ended up walking together," she said. "We had great craic because we have a lot of shared interests and plenty in common." By the time the ten-day trip was coming to an end Liz and Philip's relationship hadn't progressed beyond the pals' stage. "I wasn't sure if he fancied me or not," she said. On the final night of the trip, while on a cruise, Liz decided to try a tactic that a friend of hers swore by. She got up mid-conversation and marched out on deck, hoping Philip would follow her. He didn't. "After a while I went back in and he was still sitting at the table, looking bewildered. I asked him to come outside so we could talk." And that's what they did. Talk. Eventually, Liz decided to take the initiative. "It was very cheesy," she said. "I can't believe I said, 'a little less conversation, a little more action please,' but, it worked!"

Showbiz for Ugly People

Or politics as it's generally known to the rest of us. Political campaigns are another form of charity work but don't tell that to the people who work on them. Taking part in a political campaign is a bit like being in a play or a film. There's a good reason why a lot of actors have affairs with their co-stars, directors and other people associated with the project. There's a boiler-room atmosphere around plays, films and political campaigns. Relative strangers are thrown together in close proximity, working long hours under pressure and ultimately the public votes – the show is a success, the film grosses trillions, the candidate is elected to office. During the rehearsal/ campaign people have to get very close very quickly. It's a great way to get to know someone; you see them under pressure and at their very worst. By the way, the 'ugly people' are the politicians, babe, not you.

The Gym

The gym has always been a great place to scope out talent. And you have the added bonus of seeing exactly what's on offer. Like any other place, regular attendance increases your chances of getting to know other people. Not only are you getting fit in the process but recent studies suggest that going to the gym regularly or even *saying* you do makes you more attractive to the male of the species.

This makes sense. I know I'd be a lot more drawn to a man who says he spends his spare time training for the marathon than one who says his favourite leisure activity is watching footie on the telly, drinking beer, belching and farting.

The Supermarket

It's more than easy to spot a single man by the contents of his basket, *shopping* basket, babe. Some dating guides suggest that you utilise the contents of the fruit and vegetable aisle as props in grocery-shop flirting. Stroking cucumbers and fondling melons is all well and good if you're auditioning for a part in some Benny Hill type revue. If you aren't, I'd strongly advise against incorporating innocent vegetables and fruit into your mating ritual at this point – plenty of time for that sort of carry-on later. Overly sexualised messing in the vegetable aisle will scare the living bejaysus out of any half-normal men.

Seriously, imagine some fella started getting suggestive with a selection of plums while you are trying to decide between broccoli and cauliflower? Exactly. On the other hand if you regularly run into the same guy in the tinned soup aisle or by the digestive biscuits then feel free to give him a friendly smile and a hello. (The same goes for men you see regularly at the bus stop, the launderette etc.)

Bookshops & Book Readings

We all have a favourite writer and it's always a treat to be able to see them in person at a book signing or reading. Think on. Is your preferred author one that appeals equally to both genders? If you're heavily into Chick Lit, great, but don't go to a reading expecting to score. Thrillers and Lad Lit are a far better bet so keep your eyes on the paper to see who's doing a reading near you.

Apart from author signings and readings, bookshops, especially those with in-house cafés are always a good place to meet fellas. There's never an available space in the cafés; you have no choice but to share a table. It may as well be with an attractive man, right?

12-Step Programmes

Yes, 12-step programmes. If you don't have an issue with drugs, alcohol, compulsive spending or gambling to name just a few of the illnesses that have 12-Step organisations associated with them (N.A. – Narcotics Anonymous, A.A. – Alcoholics

Anonymous, G.A. – Gamblers Anonymous and D.A. –
Debtors Anonymous), I am not for a second suggesting that
you trot along to the nearest church basement and make up
a tale of woe just to see if there are any fanciable fellas in the
vicinity.

Do bear two things in mind. There are a myriad of 12-step
Organisations around including those for the family, friends
and spouses of alcoholics – AlAnon; adult children of
alcoholics – ACOA, as well as Overeaters, Sex Addicts,
Shopaholics, and co-dependants.

If there are no 12-Step programmes around that are appropriate
to you, either personally or by association, then you are

A. Perfect
B. Lying, or
C. A bunch of women with wands showed
     up at your christening.

The second thing to bear in mind about 12-step
organisations is that you might be in need of visiting one
anyway. A.A. is probably the best known of all the 12-Step
groups not only because it was the first but because alcoholism
isn't exactly a rarity.

If you think you have an issue with drink (or anything else)
don't resist taking action until after you meet someone. Why?

A. The boy you take up with is quite likely to be a
     serious jarhead himself.

B. If you are getting severely scuttered on a regular

44

basis the sort of fella you'll attract is unlikely to be a nurturing supportive chap.

C. It's far easier to tackle serious personal issues when you have only your own set to deal with.

D. Catting around when you are half or fully scuttered isn't a good idea because you are more likely to take stupid risks with your health and/or safety.

A lot of women think that if they quit drinking their life will be over and they'll never have intimate relations with a man again. This is quite simply untrue. OK, having told you that, I should admit that giving up the drink had a discernible impact on my own love life. IT GOT BETTER.

Obviously, the primary reason for going to any self-help organisation or 12-Step programme should be getting help for a specific problem. If you do find yourself banged up in rehab then you need to work on some other stuff before worrying about relationships. Apart from that as any celeb-stalker magazine worth its salt will tell you, Rehab Relationships are never a good idea.

Weddings

According to the old cliché 'the going to one wedding is the making of another'. Quite right too. Weddings are about the only time a person assembles all of their friends and relations under one roof. During the course of the couple's courtship you may have met some of the groom's single friends – but certainly not all of them. And then there's his gorgeous cousin just back from a year in Australia.

Needless to say, you are well prepared and looking stunning in the fancy rig-out you bought specially for the occasion.

> When Grainne got married she was determined to match-make between Alannah, one of her best friends, and Pete, the Best Man. Unfortunately Grainne's efforts were somewhat undermined when Pete spent the better part of the reception getting off with Miriam. Two years on and Pete and Miriam are living together.

Amateur Drama and Acting Class

Amateur Drama (AmDram) and Acting Classes tend to attract both men and women in roughly equal numbers. If you are a frustrated thespian then get signed up for the local theatre group or classes. If you have no desire to tread the boards, get along to the local dramatic society as fast as you can. Everybody, and I mean everybody, involved in AmDram seems to think they're Judy Garland in *A Star Is Born* (even the boys). The most hotly contested roles are those backstage and front-of-house because nobody wants to do them. If you turn up volunteering to pull curtains or sell tickets, you will be instantly popular.

Acting classes are a good idea even if you have no ambitions for a career in the limelight. An acting class is a great way of meeting a wide variety of people. Due to the interactive nature of the exercises you have no choice but to break through the ice very quickly and get to know your classmates.

Attending an acting class is particularly worth considering if you are in any way shy. Now I know at first glance this sounds like telling someone who's scared of heights to take a trip to the top of the Empire State Building. It isn't. In a beginners' class everyone is in the same boat and equally nervous. You are not going to be flung on to the stage of the Abbey Theatre at the end of the class. The exercises in a beginners' acting class are usually pretty rudimentary and great fun.

Of course, with both AmDram and acting classes you run the risk of getting off with an actor — just don't say you haven't been warned.

Art Galleries and Museums

So you know nothing about art, antiques or antiquities — Big Deal. It's not important. Things in museums are there to look at. They usually have a handy piece of cardboard attached to them explaining what they are, so you won't be ignorant for long. Walking around looking at the exhibits is one way of bumping into people. The other is to attend a lecture or talk at the institution. Most galleries and museums have a full programme of events. Check their website, or sign up for the newsletter to see what talks are lined up for the next couple of months.

Don't just go to a lecture for the sake of going. Pick a topic that you find interesting or alternatively one you know nothing about but *want* to know about. That way if you walk away at the end of the evening with nothing more than enlightenment on the difference between Ionic and Corinthian columns, then your time will have been well spent. On top of that, going to a lecture or talk will give you something to talk about other than what happened on *Emmerdale* this week.

Museum and Gallery coffee shops are a great place to meet

47

members of the opposite sex.

Flash The Ash

Now look, if you don't smoke then don't start. If you do, then give up. OK, my moral obligations regarding cigarettes have now been met. If you do smoke, then you'll already know what I'm about to tell you. Since pubs in Ireland and New York introduced the smoking ban, a whole new dating scene has emerged. Fag-breaks outside the local are no longer just a place to fill your lungs with nicotine and tar, but also to meet fellas who have a similar interest. I have met all kinds of interesting people – not just fellas, while huddled in doorways trying to inhale as much smoke as I could before I contracted hypothermia, (the temperature in NY regularly drops to below freezing during the winter months). Like all outcasts, we smokers have an instant bond, an instant subject on which we agree and nothing better to do than chat to each other while we get our fix.

A Field Guide to the Irish Male

The Candidate

How to Spot Him:

The candidate would wear a suit to the beach if he had time to go but he's far too busy handing out leaflets and making speeches. He cares deeply about 'the people' but stiffs waitresses on tips. His house is a kip because he's far too preoccupied with important world affairs to do anything as pedestrian as wash dishes.

Habitat:

On your doorstep when you are trying to have your tea or watch *EastEnders*. Outside Mass indiscriminately shaking hands. The supermarket, cattle fairs, school sports days and several other places he won't be seen in again – until the next election.

What he says:

"I know I can count on your number 1 in the by-election." "Just stick it in a brown envelope and say nothing." "Ask not what the party can do for you but what you can do for the party." Quotes extensively (and very annoyingly) from *The West Wing*.

What you'll never hear him say:

"Politics is showbiz for ugly people."

Chapter Six

Don't Leave Home Without...

Sometimes you don't have to venture far to find a fella

Every rule has its exception and here's mine. Nine times out of ten if you want to meet a fella you need to get out of the house. However, there are a few alternatives that don't involve straying too far from your sofa.

Trash & Treasure

One woman's *Trash* is another woman's *Treasure*, or so the theory goes. Unlike a lot of theories this one has a practical application. Trash & Treasure parties are a great way to meet eligible men and to score brownie points with your friends at the same time. Basically you get together with three or four other single women. Arrange a dinner, either in someone's home or a restaurant. Each girl brings along a single guy that she has no interest in – he could be an ex, a co-worker, a family member, or her next-door neighbour. That way you all get to meet three or four available fellas. Given those odds, someone is bound to score.

51

OK, having said that, I would like to add a word of caution here. Be very sure how you feel about the single chap you bring along to a Trash & Treasure party. You might be one of those girls who doesn't see the potential in a guy until he starts hitting it off with another girl.

> *A few years back Cathy went to a T&T shindig. For weeks before the do Cathy's friend Mary Alice kept going on about the chap she was bringing, saying how perfect he would be for Cathy. When the big night came Cathy wasn't all that taken with the chap in question although he seemed to be more than smitten with her. However, the more attention he paid Cathy, the more annoyed Mary Alice got. When the party ended Mary Alice made a nasty remark to Cathy and left in high dudgeon. Guess what? Mary Alice has been doing a line with the chap since.*

If you and your friends do decide to have a Trash & Treasure night there is one rule I'd suggest you adhere to very strictly. If the single man you are bringing along cannot make it and you can't find a good substitute in time then DON'T GO. I know it's a pain in the bum if you are left high and dry on a Friday night while all your friends are otherwise occupied. However, a night in alone won't kill you and it's a damn sight better than falling out with a close friend or associate over a boy.

Home Delivery

As more and more luxury apartment complexes spring up around the country (as opposed to the grotty bed-sit tenements of the past), the scope for running into your neighbours goes beyond chance meetings by the front door or postbox. If your building has a laundry or (lucky you) a gym, remember that these two rooms provide you with a damn-sight more than an opportunity to clean your sheets or work on your pecs.

Now although your apartment building might prove to be a good hunting ground, like work you need to be very careful how you proceed (see *Working It*). Jumping in at the deep end with the good-looking guy who lives across the hall is all well and good until it goes pear-shaped. Tread lightly; remember this is a guy you're going to run into regularly.

If you rugby tackle him to the sofa and attempt to jump him and he rebuffs your advances, think how you're going to feel every time you come out of your flat and see his door, never mind him. If you rugby tackle him to the sofa and he responds but legs it home before you wake up the next morning and makes no moves to follow up, how will that make you feel when you see him coming home with another girl? If you fancy your neighbour, it's best to proceed as friends until you get some notion of how he feels about you. Honestly, deferring gratification in this case will save you a whole bunch of bother down the line, not to mention the hassle of moving again.

Closer to Home

I know two couples who met when they were sharing an apartment. One couple has been happily married for over ten years. The second couple had a baby and broke up soon after. Dating your flatmate is a dodgy business, mainly because you never actually *date* them. You live together so you hang out a lot anyway and the 'dating' usually starts in bed. This is fine as long as you stay together but when you break up . . . One girl I know started going out with her flatmate soon after he moved in. Three months later he stopped sharing her bed but continued to share the rent. She was devastated as she was still mad about him. Worse again, she couldn't move on when she was seeing him every day. Eventually when he took another girl home she realised it was time for him to move out.

A Field Guide to the Irish Male

Feathery Stroker

How to Spot Him:

When he's not out hugging trees and harassing small furry animals, the Feathery Stroker likes leading nature walks and sipping herbal tea in a biodegradable café. He's usually on the skinny side and has skin that's best kept out of the sun.

Habitat:

Vegetarian restaurants, ecology protests, relationship counselling and running around in the nip at men's consciousness-raising weekends in the woods.

What he says:

"Actually I'm a bit of a feminist myself."

What you'll never hear him say:

"Real men don't cry." "I'll have that steak rare."

Chapter Seven

The Longest Journey Starts . . .

Playing Away

Planes, Trains and Automobiles

Travel, it's said, broadens the mind. It can also enhance your romantic life no end. Long-distance journeys, by plane, train or bus are great for getting to know someone. If for no other reason, the boredom of being trapped in a seat for five hours or more will drive even the shyest of people to talk to the person beside them.

Roisin travels a lot for her job. In the past she has dated two men that she met on aeroplanes. The first guy wasn't even sitting beside her but was on the other side of the aisle. When she was putting her bag in the overhead bin she noticed what he was reading and asked him what he thought of the book. They began to talk about the book, the author and five hours later when the plane landed they exchanged telephone numbers and agreed to meet for dinner. Boy number two was sitting beside her on another flight; they got chatting and subsequently dated for six months.

56

You don't even have to sit beside them on the plane. A few years back I got delayed on a stop-over because of bad weather. The airline company instead of leaving us all to investigate the duty-free and over-priced snack bars got us to the gate under false pretences. We were all stuck there like eejits for hours with no sign of the plane taking off. Girls, note this for future reference. Nothing unites people like adversity. All over the departure lounge total strangers were venting to other total strangers. Somewhere in the middle of all of this I got chatting to a very good-looking Danish man who lived in New York. We weren't sitting anywhere near each other on the plane but he dropped by my seat a couple of times during the flight. On his last visit he gave me his card and asked me to call him. I was in the middle of breaking up with someone and felt too overwhelmed by everything to start dating someone else so I never called him. I should have. What would it have cost me to meet him for a drink or dinner?

Whenever you take a trip (and don't rule out short journeys either) go prepared. Have a business card at the ready so when you are parting from your new best friend and possible future boyfriend you can just hand him your card with a minimum amount of fuss. That's all there is to it.

"Oh no, I'd be morto."

No, you wouldn't. This is a total stranger whom you may never see again, and if you do it'll probably be because he did call you. You lose nothing by doing this, absolutely nothing.

When Ciara was getting nowhere with the cute boy in the off-licence despite purchasing wine so often that her flat looked like a small pub, she decided to take the initiative.

57

Ciara figured she had nothing to lose, if off-licence-boy said no. She didn't have to go back into the shop, especially as she already had more than enough wine at home to keep her going for years. On the contrary she had plenty to gain — not least her bank balance might get a chance to recover from all of the unwarranted spending on booze.

As it happened the boy in the off-licence is now her husband. After they started dating he told her that he had no intention of ever asking her out — he was sure she would turn him down.

Unlikely as it seems, your car may be the catalyst in meeting a fella.

Jenny met her husband when he rear-ended her at a traffic lights. In Paula's case she was the one who went into the back of another car. Even though the other car was unharmed and the driver uninjured he started to threaten Paula, who, understandably worried about her safety, called the guards. "One of them was just gorgeous," Paula said. "Really lovely." A few months later Paula had her handbag stolen and when she went to the station to report the incident it was the same guard that took her statement. For two weeks after she'd had her bag stolen Paula drove her friends demented talking about the tall good-looking guardian of the peace. Eventually one of her friends put the phone in her hand and said, "Either call him, or shut up." Paula made the call, they went out and the rest is history.

Not Ferry Nice

Now although I have heard third-hand accounts of girls finding love en route to Holyhead it hasn't been my experience. Granted you do get a lot more freedom of movement on a ferry hence increased opportunities to meet members of the opposite sex. Mind you, from what I can remember, unless you're in the market for a very drunk puking chap then the chances of striking it lucky are slim. But hey, who knows. I know one girl whose parents met over a septic tank. Cupid isn't picky about where he shoots his arrows.

Home Work

OK, so you're flat out broke. You haven't got the dosh for an exotic holiday or even a long weekend within driving distance. OK, but that's still no excuse for sitting home with the TV guide and a crate of Mars Bars. Most of us, when we go on holiday, kill ourselves to see *all* of the sights. Meanwhile we neglect those on our doorsteps that other people travel thousands of miles to see. Take a bus tour of your home town (or the nearest large one). Make a list of all the museums and galleries that are close by and you've never visited. Then GO.

> *Imelda was quite happy being a lawyer in her native Derry until she decided to visit some of the local sights on her day off. She got chatting to an American tourist and two years later she's married, living in New York and making her living as an actor. All because she decided to take an interest in local history!*

Bigger towns and cities usually have a variety of tours — historical, literary, music, architectural, and pub crawls disguised as culture. Walking tours in particular are a great way of meeting new people.

A Field Guide to the Irish Male

The Guru

How to Spot Him:

He bears a striking resemblance to Rasputin, with mad long matted hair and an even madder beard. The Guru has a casual approach to personal hygiene so you may well know he's around before you even see him. He wears open-toed sandals all the time, even when there's a foot of snow on the ground.

Habitat:

Hippie communes, anywhere people are firing up a doobie, ashrams and the folks' back bedroom (when he's between trips).

What he says:

"When I was studying in India with the Swami." "Good blow, man."

What you'll never hear him say:

"Where could I purchase a tie and some aftershave?"

61

Chapter Eight

Striking a Match

When you need help finding a flame: The Internet, Speed Dating and Professional Matchmakers

Dating Agencies and Matchmakers

Like anything else that involves an exchange of cash (yours) for a service, you need to do your homework. Find out how long the agency has been around. You don't want to hand over your savings to a fly-by-night effort.

Ask the agency for referrals. They might show you written testimonials; these are fine as long as you can actually contact the people who wrote them. If they are as good as they say they are, then there will be plenty of satisfied customers only too eager to sing their praises.

If you join an agency and they fail to provide you with suitable dates – complain. There is no guarantee that you're going to meet the man of your dreams but if you supply them with a specific criteria – for example professional men between 35 and 45, who are no shorter than 5' 10" and they consistently ignore your request by setting you up with aging farmers who wouldn't reach the cow's armpit, then you have grounds for complaint.

> *Aoife went to a very expensive dating agency a couple of years ago. Her experience was not a good one. Part of the reason the agency was so pricey was because it promised that a dedicated matchmaker would personally pair Aoife with the most suitable dates. Aoife paid four figures for ten matches but gave up after number eight. "It was just a factory," she said. "The men I was meeting weren't at all suitable for me. I have no doubt that they were not, as the agency had promised, being carefully screened. I think they were just picked at random. The whole experience was terribly disappointing."*

Aoife decided she could pick better dates for herself at a fraction of the cost via the Internet. Remember you are paying for a service (in some cases paying a hell of a lot of money) so you are entitled to get what you ask for. If an agency deliver on your specific criteria and you don't click with any of the candidates then that's not their fault, and you can't expect them to do any more for you.

The Internet, Love at First Byte

What can I say – was there ever a better time to be single? Some people still persist in thinking that dating agencies, whether of the cyber or terrestrial variety, are for losers. Right. If Internet dating were for losers it would no longer exist. Instead it is a multi-million-dollar industry.

> *Aoife started by going to the personals section of her online provider, a move that cost her nothing. She replied to three*

Love at First Byte

postings and got a reply from one. "To this day," she said, "it was the most amazing correspondence I've had with anyone, ever." After exchanging "amazing" emails for a while Aoife and the guy decided to meet in person. They ended up dating for three months but her new BF who was in his early thirties and just coming out of a nine-year marriage wasn't ready for a commitment. "He was totally up front and honest about it," Aoife said. "He didn't string me along and I really appreciated it."

Undeterred, Aoife who was in her mid-thirties at the time, joined an on-line dating service and posted a profile. "I wanted to get married and have children and I wanted to know that if I got to forty-five and hadn't done either, that at least I'd done my best and put myself out there." Aoife found on-line dating ideal as she is partially deaf and found it difficult to interact with men in bars or at parties. "It's hard to flirt and be entertaining when you're constantly having to say, "I'm sorry. What was that?" "Sorry, could you repeat that again." It kinda spoils the moment and makes it hard to make a good first impression."

After meeting about forty different men Aoife had a date with Tim. "He was the only one I agreed to have a second date with," she said. Reader, she married him. Tim's sister, who was in her mid-forties, divorced with three children and convinced that she would never meet anyone again, was so impressed with his success that she signed up to an on-line dating service. A year later she too married someone she met on-line.

Aoife had a very positive experience with Internet dating. "I got to go plenty of bars and restaurants I wouldn't have gone to otherwise," she said. "I didn't meet anyone who you would call weird and everyone I met was pretty much the way they'd described themselves in their profiles. Some people have bad things to say about the Internet but I think they gave up too easily. I mean if you went to a bar and didn't meet someone you wouldn't steer clear of bars for the rest of your life, would you?"

As you would expect, no sooner had Aoife met Tim, than the Internet yielded another great man. "Typical," she commented. "He was really lovely. If it hadn't been for Tim . . ."

Not everyone who uses online dating sites is looking for a husband. Aoife was and chose to date only men who were after a LTR. This is the great thing about the Internet; it gives boys and girls an opportunity to state up front whether they are looking for love or just a quick fling. Unlike Aoife, Saoirse isn't all that interested in settling down and uses on-line dating services to ensure that she's never bored.

"It goes in waves," Saoirse said about on-line dating. "In the winter it's pretty lousy but come the spring…" Saoirse has two jobs and doesn't have a lot of spare time so she really likes the fact that she can go out every time she has a night free, "on my terms". She subscribes to two dating sites. One works like a traditional matchmaker and chooses partners based on your answers to a questionnaire. The second site is one where people just post their profiles and respond to others as and when they want.

"I've met some really great people on-line over the past three years," Saoirse said. "OK, I've met some creeps as well, but overall it's great otherwise I wouldn't still be doing it. It really is one of the best ways to meet people especially if you're really busy and don't have time to waste."

The wonderful thing about Internet dating is how specific it

---

is. This is *Precision Dating* at its finest – you can narrow your options by age, income, religion, even to whether someone is pet-friendly or not. Most importantly you are instantly privy to the amount of commitment a chap is looking for. A quick glance at any on-line dating site will give you a clue about just how many single men there are out there.

Passive or Active

You can approach Internet dating in two ways. Passive is the easiest option for someone who is going on to the Internet for the first time and is a bit scared by the whole concept. Passive Internet dating is basically checking other people's postings and replying to them. With this strategy, it's all about quantity. The more postings you respond to the more chance you have of getting responses. Throw the net wide. You feel a little so-so about someone; the hell with it, just drop them a line. It's an email, babe, not a commitment ceremony.

Chances are that not every one you approach is going to respond to you. Do not let this deter you. Fiona went on-line once and replied to a single posting. The guy didn't respond and she wrote off the entire thing as a waste of time. After one go.

Active Internet dating means putting up a posting yourself. Doing this seriously increases your chances of meeting someone. Most sites ask for a profile and a photo. Both are important. Think of yourself as a hot-shot ad agent trying to sell a product. The profile is your sales pitch. It has to say 'choose me'.

I know a lot of girls who will just stop here. The prospect of having to string a few words together is utterly terrifying. Fair enough, not everyone can write sales pitches. If you

don't feel up to doing your own profile then rope in a friend.
Which of your friend's emails do you always open first? Then
this is your girl (or it could be a fella). Even if you are good at
writing it might be a good exercise to get a friend to write the
profile anyway – just to see what they say. Your friends will see
qualities in you that you don't see in yourself. Also, don't
discount the opinions of an ex. Obviously an ex you are still
on good terms with, not one whose heart you broke. His
comments might not be all that appropriate!

Checking Out Other Chicks

Check other girls' profiles to see how they present
themselves. If you know someone who has a posting on a
dating site ask them what their response level is like and then
use their profile as a guide. Another factor to consider when
you're writing your profile is which guys' profiles you
responded to. Not the pictures, woman, what they said about
themselves. Were they funny? Simple? Mysterious?

Aoife got plenty of response to her on-line profile because
she included quite a few 'talking points' such as "I've
jumped out of an aeroplane and once stood in the same lift
as Bono".

Whoever pens the profile the abiding rule is this –
DON'T LIE

If you are 5' 4" and slightly pudgy with mousy brown hair,
fine; just don't describe yourself as a svelte and leggy blonde.
The leggy blonde will get dozens of responses but what do you
think will happen when you organise a date and the leggy
blonde turns out to be not-so-leggy and not blonde? Exactly.

Brid's Internet date described himself as a well-built blond. They arranged to meet in the café of a bookshop. Adonis said she'd know him by his leather jacket and motorcycle helmet (how macho!). Brid is no eejit, so when she arrived she decided to do a bit of reconnaissance from behind a bookshelf. There was a fella sitting in the café wearing a black leather jacket with a motor cycle helmet placed on the table beside his fluffy coffee. He was blond all right, or so the few wisps of hair on his otherwise bald pate suggested and as for being well built — "stout is how I'd put it, and that's being polite," Brid reported. She didn't hang around to see if he had a nice personality because he had already demonstrated that he was either A. deluded or B. a big fat hairy liar or C. a combination of both. Who can blame her?

Way Too Much Information

On the other hand don't feel honour-bound to offer up every grim and grisly detail of your life to date in your on-line profile. Keep it light, keep it simple, and give enough details to spark someone's interest.

Ran the marathon? YES.
Been involved in one or more road accidents? NO.
Got a funny/quirky story? YES
Been married and divorced several times? NO.

Snap Happy

It's harder to lie about your appearance when you have to post a photograph. Hard but not entirely impossible. If the site you join has the space for a photo don't even bother writing the profile if you are not prepared to supply a visual.

You are ten times more likely to get a response with a photo than without one.

Think about it. If you are looking at boys' profiles and one of them doesn't have a picture what do you think?

He could be – shy.

He could be – ashamed (afraid of his friends, family or HIS WIFE, seeing his photo on–line) If he's single and doesn't want his friends or family seeing him on–line you do not want to know him, you want a guy with a bit of backbone.

He could be – lying. "I'm a 6'4" Adonis aged 35 but if you saw my photo you'd know I'm a prematurely bald 42-year-old with a beer belly."

Or if you're anything like me you assume that he's the Elephant Man's younger uglier brother and scroll down to the next fella.

"I'm ready for my close-up"

Take the same care and attention with the photo that you took writing your profile. Don't just scan in any ould snap-shot of yourself that's handy. You don't have to take weeks to decide on the right photograph but you should put a bit of time and effort into selecting one. Obviously it should be a current photo. If you are 33 with red hair and a size 12, don't put in a picture of yourself at 22 with peroxide blonde hair when you were a size 8.

More and more people are opting to get pictures done specially for their web posting and this is a very good idea.

Going to a professional photographer is one option. Think about it. Even girls that are naturally photogenic – Giselle, Kate, Elle and the like, need a little help. Those lassies spend hours with hairdressers, makeup artists and lighting experts. They don't just wander into work and say to the photographer, 'get to snapping'. Even with all the hours of preparation those photos still get retouched. Think on.

If cash is tight then wait until you've had your hair done, put on a bit of make-up and get a friend to take the picture. However, don't go overboard. You want the picture to be representative of how you look, so keep the look as natural as possible. Big hair and too much make-up is fine for drag queens but you don't want to be mistaken for someone whose professional name is Miss Carriage of Justice or Miss L. Toe, now do you?

Keep your pose as natural as possible also. Overly-posed sultry come-hither Liz Hurley-type efforts will certainly attract a lot of attention. That's fine if you're in the market for a well-dodgy geezer.

The (real) Rules

The Internet gets a lot of bad press. Media outlets love stories about serial killers and paedophiles who lure victims through the medium of cyberspace. These things do happen but don't forget that plenty of people go on-line without disastrous consequences. In fact, many people go on-line and end up in nice relationships or even married to perfectly normal non-serial killer non-paedophile men. Unfortunately those are not the types of stories which make good headlines so we're only ever likely to hear about the bad stuff.

There are some ground rules that will help screen out any dodgy types. Do not give out any personal information such as your home telephone number, your home address, your work address or telephone number. I would even go as far as to say you shouldn't give out your mobile number until you've been in regular contact for a while.

Basic Instinct

Trust your instincts. If something feels funny, or wrong, then don't ignore it. If things don't add up, and this is true on all occasions not just on-line, then don't ignore them. A few years ago a girlfriend of mine started dating a guy who was in his early thirties. He didn't have a job — never a good sign. His explanation was that he had been in PR, with Saatchi and Saatchi and had gone as high up the corporate ladder as he could and now he was taking time off to see what his next challenge would be. This was a complete crock and like most crocks stank to high heaven. No wonder, he was lying outright. He'd never worked a day in PR never mind in Saatchi and Saatchi. He was on the dole and didn't want to let on, so he made up a story to impress girls.

Pay close attention to the information people give you. If things don't add up then there's a reason. Apart from sexual predators there are a number of unscrupulous types who will go on-line posing as being single when in actuality they aren't. When you decide you like your on-line match enough to meet him don't invite him to your home or go to his. I don't care how plausible his reasons might be, how wonderful or perfect he appears, you are not to go to his house. Yet.

Arrange to meet in a public place, tell a friend where you

will be, who you are meeting and arrange to have them check in with you by phone. Feel free to let your date know that people know exactly where you are and who you are with. If he's kosher this will not bother him in the slightest.

Yeah, I know I'm giving your mother a run for her money, but you really cannot be too careful. If he's the ONE, then you'll find out soon enough. Meeting for coffee before you give him your home telephone will not divert the course of true love, trust me on this.

Your on-line romance should proceed in the following order:

1. Exchange Emails.
2. Exchange Phone Calls.
3. Exchange handshakes in a public place.
4. Exchange bodily fluids if appropriate.

Speed Dating

If it's quantity you're after, then Speed Dating is one of the best ways to go. If you have no idea how speed dating works, here's a quick primer. Depending on the company organising the event you have a series of 'dates' with men each lasting 3 – 8 minutes. Each participant is given a number and a score-card, (no pun intended, I'm sure). On the score-card, participants record the numbers of the people they'd like to meet again. Some companies give participants more than one category to choose from. For example 'Just Friends', 'Dating,' 'Something More'.

When the dating ends the participants go home and feed their results into the company website. When two people's choices match they are given an opportunity to communicate via emails the speed-dating organisation has given them. This ensures that you don't even have to give out your own email until you are good and ready.

I think this is just a fabulous idea. It's great fun and if you are inclined towards impatience (guilty) then this is the way to go. The first time I tried speed dating the individual dates lasted three minutes each. Sounds like no time at all, right. Well, in more than one case it seemed to stretch to infinity. Every time that happened I offered up a silent prayer of thanks that I hadn't gone on a 'real' date with the chap in question.

The second speed-dating event I went to had dates that lasted eight minutes each and I didn't like it as much as the first time. Eight minutes is a really long time when you've got nothing to say to the person sitting opposite you. Also because of the increased length of time of the individual dates you don't get to meet as many guys. As I said before, when you're in the business of looking for a boy, it's quantity that counts. As they say on Wall St. "Churn 'em and burn 'em." Ultimately it all depends on the individual. I'm sure some girls would be more comfortable with eight minutes than three and vice versa.

A lot of girls (and guys) go to speed-dating events alone and this is OK. However, if possible I would recommend going with at least one other girl – that way you can make a night of it and more importantly compare notes on your 'dates'. If nothing else you'll have a good laugh. Also, if you want to go out afterwards with someone you met at the event you can all go together as a group.

A Field Guide to the Irish Male

Captain Tightfist

How to Spot Him:

Captain Tightfist is a bit of a chameleon; he's well able to blend in to the general population – until the bill comes. Then he shows his true colours. Captain Tightfist would rather run naked down Grafton Street on a Saturday afternoon than part with cash. He doesn't mind spending money, as long as it's not his own. He never leaves home without his pocket calculator. He is always first out of the taxi and last up to the bar. He is the man who will only allow the fairy lights on the Christmas Tree to be lit for a few hours on Christmas Day, because he's worried about the electricity bill.

Habitat:

At home checking his bank accounts on-line. Sprinting from taxis, hovering in the bathroom when the bill arrives.

What he says:

"You had a Diet Coke and two breadsticks so that means you owe . . ."

What you'll never hear him say:

"The drinks are on me."

Chapter Nine

Working It

Finding the right boy needn't always be hard graft

Labour of Love

Loads of people meet their partners at work. In a way this makes complete sense. Let's face it, we all see a lot more of our colleagues than we do our family or friends. Mind you, dating in the workplace is a tricky one. I'm reminded of the old cliché about not defecating on your own doorstep. If you do fancy someone you work with, it's a good idea to hold off on the intimate relations side of things until you get an idea where things are going.

Increasingly in Ireland companies are being sued for sexual harassment. As a result many larger corporations are introducing policies and guidelines regarding relationships between members of staff, so be sure to know what, if any, official policy your company has. Apart from that, increased awareness of sexual harassment has made romances in the workplace harder than ever, so make sure you check out all your options.

1. If you work in a large company look beyond your immediate department and co-workers.

2. In a large corporation or company don't discount outside support staff, co-workers in other locations, or even clients but obviously not if it's going to damage your career prospects.

3. Business trips, conferences and expos are another great source of new talent.

With work-related liaisons the cardinal rule should always be, *don't do something which will adversely affect your career.* Unfortunately in many offices and factories the old double standard is *thriving*. It's one rule for the boys (who will be boys) and another entirely for the girls. Remember a boy is a bit of fun but a job pays the bills.

When Derval started working for a new company she didn't spend more time with her boss than was strictly necessary. "He was the boss," she said, "in other words to be avoided at all costs." About three months after she started in the firm she was heading to the 'usual Friday night piss-up', when she spotted Brian, the boss, alone at his desk. "I felt bad, because it was a small enough office and he never got asked anywhere." Derval asked Brian if he wanted to come to the pub with the rest of the gang. Brian said he couldn't as he had plans. "Don't think you can get out of buying me a drink that easily," Derval shot back. "I don't know what came over me," she said. "It wasn't like I even fancied him." Brian told her to name the time and the place and Derval arranged to meet him the following Sunday for brunch. After having brunch Derval and Brian ended up spending the entire day together. "They were calling last orders in the pub," Derval said, "we were both a bit drunk and I asked him if he was ever going to kiss me. He couldn't believe I'd actually said that, which made two of us."

Derval and Brian didn't have to keep their relationship a secret from their colleagues for very long. "It all happened very quickly," Derval said. "I got pregnant on our third date, so once I told people I was pregnant it kind of followed that they'd want to know who the Dad was." Although Derval's colleagues were generally supportive, she did notice a change in attitude. "I suppose it's only to be expected if you're going out with the boss that people will be a bit more guarded around you. More so now that we're married."

Official Office Protocol

If you do decide to have an office romance you need to be very careful about how you proceed.

DON'T tell everyone at work that you're going out with a colleague. Try it and you'll get a small taste of how celebrity couples feel having their every move scrutinised. Having said that, it's almost impossible to keep a workplace romance secret. However, what people *think* they might know, and what they actually know are two entirely different things. Let them wonder. If they're talking about you then they're leaving some other poor eejit alone.

It might be a good idea, if the hook-up looks like being longer than a fling to tell your boss in confidence. In an ideal world it's really none of her business. However, imagine what life will be like if everybody else cottons on before she does? Unpleasant doesn't begin to cover it. Bosses like to think that they know everything that's going on in the office, (they're supposed to but rarely do). Be sure that you are the one who tells management your business and not some busybody who might not have your best interests at heart.

If a relationship goes on for long enough, eventually your colleagues will find out – officially. By that time hopefully you and your partner will be established as a couple and able to put up with some curiosity without it having a negative impact on the relationship. On the other hand, do you really want to spend all day, every day, with your beloved? That kind of intensity can wreck even the strongest of partnerships. Something to think about before getting to know the cute boy from HR, right?

Heavy Petting

DON'T take your colleagues' knowledge about your workplace romance as a licence to out yourselves completely and take your relationship into the workplace. As a general rule keep the cute pet names for each other's company and no one else's.

DON'T take your PDAs (Public Displays of Affection) into or near the workplace. The office is not the place for holding hands or playing kissy face. It will make your colleagues very uncomfortable, you will be less than popular in no time at all and it won't do you any good when you're looking for a pay rise or a promotion. Unless it's the boss you're snogging and that's a whole other kettle of fish entirely.

Opportunity Ain't Knocking?

If you work in a place where the opportunities of getting off with some one are limited, like a convent, then taking a part-time job is a great way of expanding your opportunities and earning some extra money into the bargain.

If you spend all week in a same-sex office or in a very small business then working evenings and weekends in a shop, bar or restaurant, is a wonderful way of meeting a wide variety of people in a short space of time.

Risky Business

No matter how careful you are, no matter how perfect you and Paul from accounts seemed for each other, there's always the chance that your budding romance will end in tears. This is why, like getting off with one of your neighbours, you should be very very careful indeed about getting involved with someone you work with.

It's hard enough working together when everything is hunky-dory and the pair of you are mad about each other but just imagine how dreadful it would be having to sit across the room from your ex every day of the week. I can think of few things worse. Apart from anything else I can remember a few nasty break-ups from my own past that were made far more bearable by being able to throw myself into my job. I can't imagine what it would have been like if I had to face into work every day and be civil to the man who had just broken my heart, or whose own organ I had cruelly crushed.

Only once have I succumbed to the temptation of an office romance and that time it was nothing more than a fling, so when it did end, there were no shattered feelings on either side and both of us were easily able to adjust to being just colleagues again. Mind you, at the time we were having our fling we thought we were cleverly pulling the wool over everyone else's eyes. We weren't.

Local Business Associations

From what I know about business organisations, the male-to-female ratio is definitely in favour of the girls. OK, so a lot of the chaps are old and married. So what, they have sons, brothers, cousins and friends. They can introduce you to someone. DUH! At the same time you're increasing your chances of furthering your career or even starting a new one.

Evening Classes

Yes, I know it's a cliché and no woman in her right mind would sign up for an *evening class* in search of a single man. Yet still, there's plenty of evening classes populated entirely by women hoping to meet men. If you decide to take an evening class then choose one about something you actually have an interest in. If you fancy going to Italy for your holidays take a class in art appreciation, speaking Italian, the life and works of Gianni Versace or how to cook Italian food.

Only enrol in a class that will enrich you as a person or help further your career. Take a painting class or one in gourmet cookery. Don't spend money on something you have shag-all interest in simply because you *might* meet a guy. This is a serious waste of time and money.

A Field Guide to the Irish Male

The Corporate Climber

How to Spot Him:

It's not easy as he's constantly in a rush. He has a wireless headset, like Madonna, for his mobile phone and he's constantly talking about markets and switching calls. He has a second mobile in case the first one runs out of power. Although he wears a suit he's usually seen with his shirt sleeves rolled up and his tie thrown over his shoulder.

Habitat:

5am the gym. 6am in the office on the phone to Hong Kong. 7am breakfast meeting with other young Turks. Lunch is for wimps. 6pm in the wine bar. 7pm back in the office to liaise with the New York office.

What he says:

"Buy." "Sell." "Get New York on the other line, NOW."

What you'll never hear him say:

"Take time to smell the roses."

Chapter Ten

Best Friends Forever

Four-legged flirt facilitators & other faithful companions

Doggie Style

Picture it, you're walking along the road minding your own business when a man you don't know comes up to you and starts chatting. What's your first reaction? Run like hell most likely. Now picture the same scene only this time you're walking your dog. A man walks by and stops to pat the dog and generally admire him. See the difference?

Dogs are the greatest date-bait ever. Normal social barriers collapse as soon as a pooch enters the picture. You are three times more likely to strike up a conversation with a stranger when you have a dog with you because dogs give people an *excuse* to talk to each other. Likewise if you're out and about and see a cute dog on one end of a lead and an even cuter boy on the other, there is nothing wrong with you stopping to put chat on both of them.

Dog runs, parks and anywhere else people take their dog for

walkies (Dun Laoghaire pier for example) are fantastic places to meet boys. While your doggie is off sniffing other doggie's bottoms you get on with the human equivalent. There are no end to the opportunities a friendly dog will provide you with. Friendly being the operative word. You don't want a dog that's going to bite the hand off the man who might possibly feed you. If your dog needs his social skills brushed up, get him to an obedience class. Even if he doesn't, an obedience class is also a great hunting-ground for potential playmates for yourself.

Down, Boy!

At obedience classes and dog runs you are immediately in a situation with people who share your interests. As a dog-lover and former dog-owner (and hopefully future dog-owner) let me tell you, people who like dogs can bond instantly and talk for hours and hours and hours about their pets. Don't forget dog shows; these are a bit like obedience classes as pretty much everyone there has dogs as a common interest.

Apart from being wonderful ice-breakers, dogs are also great flirt facilitators. A dog gives you leave to say things you mightn't get away with otherwise. "Oh, he likes you," you say to the cutie patting your doggie on the head. "He's got good taste." Be warned, talking via your dog is fine in the initial stages of a flirtation but it gets old real fast. When you're actually going with a fella please please please refrain from saying things like, "Pookie wants Daddy to give Mummy a kiss". Why? Because it's nauseating that's why. If you haven't the balls to directly request a snog from your own boyfriend, God help the future of the relationship.

Not Just For Christmas

Another warning. A dog is for life and not just to assist your social life. Don't run out and buy a dog as soon as you read this simply because you want to pick up fellas. If you get a dog simply to meet a man, it will backfire. Any dog-loving man will spot your insincerity a mile off, so don't do it.

If you are a genuine dog-lover and without a dog of your own to walk, you can always volunteer with an animal shelter or rescue agency. This will give you boundless opportunities to meet cute guys and imagine their gratitude when you are the one responsible for setting them up with the dog of their dreams.

If you don't fancy the animal shelter, then you can volunteer to walk the dog of an elderly neighbour or family member. Or if you have time on your hands, set up your own dog-walking business. Apart from the increased opportunities walking the dog will bring, it's good exercise, helps keep you looking your best and will bring in some extra cash.

Forget man's best friend, dogs are definitely a girl's best friend.

Hidden in Plain Sight

When what you are looking for is right there in front of you all along.

Romance novels and women's magazines just love, loooooove it, when the heroine's love interest is under her nose from the very start. He's the loyal friend she takes for granted and sometimes abuses. He stands by her as she pursues a relationship with a handsome and ruthless Captain of Industry. Eventually Mr. Moneybags sweeps our girl off her feet and just as they are about to live happily ever after she discovers that he's been interfering with some other slapper all along. Just before the final curtain drops she suddenly really sees her faithful friend for the first time. And would you believe it, he's stunningly studly. They kiss. Fireworks go off. The End. Aaaaah.

Right. Stories like this are the EXCEPTIONS. For every man who supports a woman through failed relationships with other men while he stands idly by waiting for her to see that he's the one, there are another hundred who got fed up waiting for their friend to cop on, said 'sod this for a game of soldiers' and found someone else.

Don't get me wrong. I'm not saying that a lot of relationships don't start out as friendships. Many do. Those are the ones that have a better chance of surviving. However, what I am saying is that if you know a friend or acquaintance fancies you then you better act now and not keep him hanging on while you test the waters with other guys. The patient devoted man who puts his one true love first and denies himself on her behalf is a nice idea (or is it really? I think it's a bit creepy myself but that's me) but he doesn't often exist outside the pages of fiction. You cannot keep a man like this on stand-by as some sort of safety net. It's bloody unfair.

The Friend Zone

The other reason why you need to act in a reasonable time is that once someone becomes firmly fixed in the *Friend Zone* then it can be next to impossible to move the relationship along to the next level. If you are friends with a boy for a long time, and I mean friends, not just pals, then you are risking quite a lot if you try to move things to a romantic arena. Many people would rather not pursue romantic feelings if it means putting a valuable friendship at risk. What can I say? It's up to the individual. I did it once. It was a disaster. I lost not only a potential BF but one of my best friends in the process. However, our friendship was a strong one and recovered — eventually. But things between us were never as comfortable as they had been before intimate relations became part of the equation.

If you do develop feelings for a close friend and it looks as though he's game for a bit of nookie, then I'm sorry to tell you there's only one thing for it. TALK TO HIM. Yeah, I know, it's going to be miserable, uncomfortable and pure cringe-making but not half as bad as it will be if you end up in bed without a road map to the eventual outcome.

On Your Marks

So now you know the WHO and the WHERE, what's next? Well, that would be WHEN. In the next section we'll take a look at getting yourself ready mentally and physically for your assault on the dating world.

A Field Guide to the Irish Male

Holy Joe

How to Spot Him:

Holy Joe is obsessively neat and tidy. He has a wardrobe full of ganseys the Mammy knitted for him. No matter what the occasion, or the weather, he has a good pair of sturdy brown shoes on.

Habitat:

In the church, annoying the hell out of the parish priest. Volunteering in soup kitchens, annoying the hell out of the homeless. Anti-abortion rallies, annoying the hell out of everyone. He doesn't watch telly because of all of the 'irreligious tripe' on the box, but if he did Ned Flanders would be his favourite character – for all the wrong reasons.

What he says:

"What would Jesus do?"

What you'll never hear him say:

"Religion is the opiate of the people." Swear-words stronger than 'darn'.

Part Three

Getting Out there

Heading out into the dating jungle

Chapter Eleven

Famine or Feast

Having the boys eat their hearts out

From my own experience and talking to my girlfriends it seems as if there are only two romantic situations a girl can find herself in. You are either fighting off the fellas who are like wasps around jam or else they're as rare as a bottle of designer mineral water in the desert.

There's nothing in the least bit baffling about this when you think about it. Nothing will make you as un-desperate as having a fella on the go. That's why when you've got one fella interested in you a whole swarm of the brutes appear out of nowhere. So, try to emulate that relaxed attitude when times are lean boywise.

Becoming Un-desperate

OK, I'm going to sound a little bit over-therapied now but bear with me; it will be worth it in the end. The first step in un-desperation is . . . learning to love yourself.

Learning to love yourself

Yes, that's what I said, learning to love yourself, or at the very least liking yourself. Think about it. Don't you know a girl who is no oil painting, no big deal, fairly ordinary in most respects except one: she can't beat off the men with a stick. Let's call her Josie. No, there's no specific reason for calling her that. It's not as if I ever knew a girl called Josie who was pretty mundane but the fellas all loved her. Where would you get such a mad idea?

Haven't you spent evenings with your single girlfriends discussing Josie over and over again? What's Josie's attraction? Why her? What's Josie's secret? Josie is no supermodel, is she? I'm not saying Josie is thick but she's hardly Stephen Hawking. She has a spare tyre/thick ankles/thunder thighs. You know women, maybe yourself, who are skinnier, prettier, more intelligent, funnier and better paid than the Josies of this world yet she's the one who's fighting off the menfolk. What is her secret? You know it yourself. At some point in the conversation it will arise. Just as the slagging is about to become uber-toxic someone will say, 'but Josie's really nice/ great craic/lovely'. Right? Right.

This girl is happy with herself and that, babe, is the most attractive trait there is. To become technical for a minute, the mathematics of the situation are thus

Unhappiness = Discontentedness = Desperation

If you don't love yourself, if you don't much like yourself, then how can you expect anyone else to? If you persist in thinking little of yourself, the equation becomes even more complicated and self-flagellating.

A man likes me, therefore he is a complete imbecile, and therefore I do not want to go out with him.

So you don't go out with the men who want to go out with you and what happens? You either pursue men who want nothing to do with you (the fools) or you don't go out with anyone at all.

The net result? DESPERATION.

Marxist Theory

> "I wouldn't belong to any club
> that would have me as a member."
>
> GROUCHO MARX

If you apply this approach to dating, where will it lead? To the wool counter and the cat shelter. Forget Groucho, get out there and join as many clubs as you can.

So what is it that you don't like about yourself? Let's start with the obvious, the externals. The first piece of home-work is easy; you've probably done it a million times already. Take off all your clothes and view yourself in a full–length mirror. Don't try this in the changing room in A-Wear as you won't be guaranteed privacy and also the lighting in most shops is such that even Claudia Schiffer would look like a teenage hippopotamus.

The reason I'm suggesting this exercise isn't simply wanton sadism. A lot of us get fixed ideas in our head about various body parts when we're in our teens. Despite the fact that our bodies are ever changing we persist in thinking of our parts as we did when we were fourteen.

Now take a good long look at your body. Try to look at it

as if you've never seen it before. What don't you like? That's the easy part. We can all list off things we don't like about our physical appearance. But before you jump in with the list you've memorised, stop and take a good look at yourself. What do you *really* see?

Massive bum? Tummy too big? Boobs too small? Arms a bit flabby. Thighs borrowed from a baby elephant? Every girl has a different list. All right then, make your list. Keep it to five things.

1
2
3
4
5

Now what is the one thing that bothers you most?
If I woke up tomorrow and could change one thing about my body, it would be...................

Self-criticism is easy. Too easy. Here's a few things I have thought about my own body in the past.

> *My stomach would make Buddha look like an anorexic.*
> *My upper arms are big enough to build homes for refugees on.*
> *My hair is crap.*

Now for the hard part. Before you freeze to death in all your nakedness, go back the mirror and take a look at the things you like. Don't tell me there isn't anything at all you don't like about your body.

Good hair. Firm boobs. Nice legs. Pretty nose. Fantastic feet.

Flat tummy. There will be something positive you can say. Do you have five fingers and five toes? It's a start. Good girl.

Now make your list

1

2

3

4

5

What do you mean you can't think of five? Rubbish. In your entire body you cannot find five things you like? Have you looked at your ankles recently? I'm serious. I happen to have very lovely ankles. No one has ever complimented me on my ankles, I very much doubt if anyone has ever noticed my ankles, but that is not the point. I happen to like them. Now fill in the five spaces above like a good girl.

Done? Good. So what next? Well, at the risk of stating the obvious, you have to capitalise on your assets and minimise your (perceived) faults. And before you panic do remember two wondrous things.

1. Your body is covered with clothing the majority of the time.

2. The faults that you see are far bigger in your head than they are on your body and they hardly exist at all for anyone else (mainly because they are far too busy worrying about their own alleged flaws).

My friend Sinead has been saving for years for a nose job.

Her nose is crooked and bumpy – according to Sinead. I have never ever heard another person refer to Sinead as 'the one with the nose' or 'her with the big crooked bumpy conk'. I have never heard anyone say a damn thing about Sinead's nose except Sinead. Sinead is, in fact, very pretty and one of the most photogenic women I know.

Fat or Phat (Pretty Hot and Tempting)?

Most women think they are overweight. Small wonder when our reference points are anorexic teen models and actresses who live on a diet of caffeine, nicotine and God knows what the doctor ordered.

What is the best way of losing weight? Crash dieting/ bulimia/cocaine/a slight touch of anorexia/all of the above. Any of these are effective at removing those excess pounds and, as an added bonus, every ounce of self-esteem you ever possessed will also vanish. Horray. Magic. Eventually you will be skinny, empty of nourishment, and quite possibly as high as a kite. This is not the way to go, babe. Ultimately you will feel, in a word, shite.

If your health and mental wellbeing aren't reason enough to stop you sticking your fingers down your throat, then let me just add, it wrecks your skin. Starvation and purging will leave you looking aged far before your time. Once this happens there is very little that will reverse it, except surgery and even that isn't guaranteed to help. The other guaranteed side effect of excessive puking is wrecked and rotten teeth.

Eating is important for overall wellbeing and good skin. Food is your friend, not your enemy. Eating properly is as much about taking care of yourself as looking both ways before you cross the road is. A girl who cares about herself will make sure she gets proper nourishment. She won't fill her body with crap that will clog her arteries, increase her blood pressure and leave her looking like a pre-menstrual Michelin Man.

Worried about weight? If you eat properly you needn't be. Look, I'm not suggesting that you subsist on nuts and grains for the rest of your existence. A healthy diet does not equal deprivation, or boredom. And if you refuse to give up chocolate, (and I for one can't blame you there) then exercise more. Go to the gym. Buy a dog and walk its tiny paws off. (Dogs are also a good way of meeting the opposite sex see *Doggie Style*). Apart from anything else, regular exercise releases endorphins which make you feel good about yourself.

Your body and health are important. If you were going for an interview for a job you really wanted you'd buy a new suit, right? So the same applies here. Set reasonable standards, if you currently look like a Sumo Wrestler then don't expect to look like Elle McPherson after a couple of goes on the Stairmaster.

Do Not Stress

Nothing reeks worse than eau de desperation. It's one of those awful paradoxes that rule life; if you desperately want a man the more likely you are to stay desperate. Let's try a little role reversal here.

What is it that generally attracts you to a man? His physical appearance? His sense of humour? The size of his wallet? The size of his endowment? All of the above? But what is it that singles out one reasonably attractive fairly funny man with large assets (financial and other) from all the others? Aren't you always that bit more interested in the one who doesn't trip over himself to get to you? The chap that appears to be happy enough to either talk to you or not to talk to you. If a fella is all over you like a rash, your first reaction isn't likely to be reaching for a pen to give him your number; more likely you will reach for the chamomile lotion to get rid of the itch. So what happens when one of these over-eager needy-weedy salivating puppy dogs asks you out? If you deign to answer him at all the reply will most likely be *'if you were the last man alive, I'd become a lesbian'*.

Remember this when you see a man you like and would like to get to know better. *Less is More.* But that doesn't mean auditioning for the role of Ice Queen. Remember to smile and give a few hints that you are agreeable to furthering the acquaintance. See, girls, it's a tricky game. Too much and they run away; too little and they think you're not interested. Life would be so much easier if our emotions appeared on our T-shirts like slogans . . . Well, maybe not. If our every feeling appeared in bold lettering for the entire world to see, few of us would still have our jobs at the end of the day.

Give Her an Oscar

Let's leave the signal strategy for a moment and get back to basics. How to act un-desperate when you're not feeling all that confident. OK, first the bad news. It is nigh on impossible to appear un-desperate. Years of method training in the Gaiety School of Acting will make no difference what-so-ever, so save your money and buy a nice handbag instead.

But wait now. Don't panic, I haven't sentenced you to a solo lifetime of knitting booties for your cat, Tesco meals for one and *Corrie* for company. Take a deep breath and read on. It is extremely hard to *act* un-desperate but it isn't all that hard to *become* un-desperate. It takes a little bit of work but then everything in life that's worth having does. If you are afeared of a little toil then I humbly suggest you stay single. All relationships need work and constant maintenance, but I'm getting ahead of myself again.

Expect Good Things.
People who expect good things are generally luckier than those who don't.

Hope is a self-fulfilling prophecy. After all what exactly is luck? Luck is being in the right place at the right time. When you read about the latest 'overnight success', you can bet your ass that they worked hard for years before being discovered as the next big thing in comedy/acting/singing – unless of course they're a boy band or a contestant on *Big Brother*.

There's no tax on thoughts, baby!

Lucky people are generally ones who work hard to provide themselves with as many opportunities as they can. This applies to everything across the board. Everyone knows a couple who bought a wonderful house at a bargain price. Yes, they did, after six months of scouring the property section and getting up every weekend at 6am to traipse around the country looking at dodgy des reses. Did they give up, stay in bed and say it'll never happen? Did they hell!

The corollary is also true, if you expect the worst then be

prepared to give a warm welcome to bad luck. Being prepared for the worst isn't the same as expecting it.

Being prepared is knowing that things can go wrong and having a back up plan.

Expecting the worst is just giving in to hopelessness and not even trying to make good things happen.

Think **BIG.**
Think **HAPPY.**
Think **HOPEFUL.**

A Field Guide to the Irish Male

Narcissus

How to Spot Him:

He's hard to miss as he's drop-dead gorgeous, but that beauty isn't down to nature alone. Narcissus has so many PCPs (Personal Care Products) that he has had to convert the spare room into a walk-in storage space for them.

Habitat:

Anywhere there is a mirror to admire himself. Although Narcissus cannot walk by a shop window without stopping, he couldn't tell you what the window display was because he was admiring his own reflection. He's rarely home as he has to make regular and frequent visits to his hairdresser, his manicurist, his personal shopper, his dermatologist, his nutritionist and his personal trainer.

What he says:

"God, you're beautiful" to his own reflection.

What you'll never hear him say:

"Looks aren't important."

Chapter Twelve

"I'm the last pre-packaged lasagne in Tesco"

Everybody wants the last lasagne and only one lucky bastard is going to get it

Chill Cabinet Chill-Out

If most of your friends are already in relationships, don't fall into the trap of thinking that life is a race and they're furlongs ahead of you. OK, so in your mind you might be the last pre-packaged lasagne in Tesco, sitting there alone on the wintry shelf of the chill cabinet. All the other pre-packaged lasagnes are gone and any second now your sell-by date will be up.

For the love of God, get a grip. Haven't you ever gone running into the supermarket at the eleventh hour thinking that all the good stuff will be gone? Aren't you always thrilled beyond belief when there's one pre-packaged lasagne left? Don't you feel lucky? Special? Blessed? Do you care that the lasagne is almost past its sell-by date? Do you hell! You have that delicious pre-prepared meal in the microwave before you can think twice and you're only thrilled with your good fortune. Remember that in moments of self-pity.

Let's take a look at those friends who you think are supposedly winning the race. They might be the lasagne that was bought early and then got stuck in the freezer only to land in the bin months later. Comparing your insides to other people's outsides is one of the biggest lessons in futility, like, EVER. It's like comparing ice cream and Wedgwood china. There is no comparison. None. No one knows what goes on in another person's head, or in fact in their relationships. Also, spending time comparing your inner life to someone else's façade (and yes, that's what it is mostly, a façade) is a ginormous waste of time. Why bother? You could be doing your nails instead. Don't do it.

Fur Coat No Knickers

As soon as you start to look at someone and think, "Oh she's so lucky", stop. You have no idea how lucky or unlucky she might be. By the same token people could be looking at you and thinking exactly the same thing. If I had a euro for every time someone has said to me, "Oh it's all right for you. You're so confident." I'd have substantially more money in my bank account then I presently do. The thing is though, until very recently I wasn't actually all that confident, just bloody good at pretending to be.

Which is exactly what I mean by *Fur Coat No Knickers*. In general people put up a front in order to get on with the business of their daily lives. You do it too. Did you honestly think you were that unique?

If you don't get over it, unfairly comparing yourself with

others will just result in yet more of that god-awful low self-esteem. Then what happens? Well, often, if you spend your time unfairly comparing yourself with every other person on the planet, you're going to feel increasingly inadequate, isolate yourself and avoid social situations. Unchecked this can lead to becoming the mad old woman with all the cats, the one the local kids swear is a witch. That's not where you want to be, is it? Didn't think so. Cut out the unfair comparisons.

How you see yourself and how others see you

You know when you look in the mirror what you see is actually the inverse of what others see. Our reflections are the wrong way around. There's a special mirror that shows people their true reflections and how they appear to the rest of the world. I have yet to hear of someone using it and not being completely horrified. It's the same when you hear your voice on tape for the first time. Show me a person who hasn't said, "God! Do I really sound like that?" and I'll show you someone who needs to have their hearing checked.

Well, guess what, babe? There's a similar gap in the way we project our personalities and the way that others perceive them. Everyone knows some bumptious old bore who cracks dreadful jokes until you want to hit him over the head with a blunt object, or indeed hit yourself over the head with a blunt object, anything, anything at all, just MAKE IT STOP.

Is this you?

The next time you are out in company take your head out of your rear and pay attention to how you behave and how others respond. Maybe you talk incessantly and don't listen to others because you're nervous. Calm down. You are with your friends. They like you.

Is the glass empty, half full or did you smash the glass to smithereens flinging it across the room in a fit of tempter?

Who Are You?

Are you a positive sort or a big moan?

In Ireland there are two things nobody ever wants said about them.

> A. They're a scab.
> B. They're no craic.

To that list let's add

> C. Being a buzz wrecker.

Everyone knows someone like this. They could whinge for Ireland in the Olympics and bring home gold, silver *and* bronze. They only have to set foot in a room and all of the joy is sucked out of the immediate atmosphere. These are people whose company you don't actively seek out and in time will actively avoid.

Could this be you? If it's not you today, are you rapidly becoming that way?

The Blame Game

It's easy to become discouraged and heaven's forbid, *bitter* when you've been on your own for a while or been Let Down a lot.

Hands up anyone who's ever uttered any of these gems.

"All the good ones are gone."

"The only fellas that ever ask me out are dirty-lookin' eejits."

"Men are all complete and utter bastards."

"Men are only interested in skinny/blonde/big-boobed girls."

"Men don't make passes at girls who wear glasses"

"Men are only after the one thing."

Oh, yeah?

If any of the statements above were true the world would be populated by blonde supermodels with perfect sight. None of us would have myopia, crooked teeth, bandy legs, love handles or frizzy hair. We'd all be extinct. We'd have been bred out of existence.

The last time I checked there were plenty of non-blonde women on the planet, some even wearing glasses. Yes, some men *are* bastards. Some gentlemen *do* prefer blondes. But for every guy that ogles the topless models on Page Three there's one who's scratching his head and saying 'big jugs don't do owt for me'.

However, that's not the point right now. The point is, project all of that negativity and you'll be proven right.

OK, babe, ever heard of a self-fulfilling prophecy? Imagine you're a guy in a café. You look over and see an attractive woman on her own. Her phone rings and you overhear the conversation. "Pricks," she's saying. "Feckin' pricks the lot of them. I wish I was a lezzer. I'm sick of them all. Wankers."

Then she catches your eye and glares at you. What are you going to do? Think 'bejaysus, me prayers are answered. Now there's a woman for me'? Doubtful.

> **The more bitchy and negative you become the less people will want you in their company and the less the chances of being introduced to someone nice.**

Keep up the bitching and you will be proved right again and again. I'm not saying you have to go through life like a lobotomised Stepford woman. Just cut out some of the negativity.

Not just about men but about life in general.

Perception

Is there a person alive who hasn't been let down at some point? Even Halle Berry had her husband publicly cheat on her. Just like death and taxes, there is no earthly protection from being let down, or in some cases, let down badly. It's normal to have feelings of grief, anger and, yes, if the occasion merits it, murderous rage. However, if you harbour those feelings, give them a lovely snug safe haven in your heart and feed them up till they become a hugely obese well nourished grudge what do you think the outcome will be?

B&T (Bitter & Twisted) that's what. Do you really need me to tell you how unattractive B&T is? No, didn't think so. OK, so you got dumped/dumped on/stood up – whatever. Yes, feel free to enjoy a bitchfest of mega proportions. Rant, rage, rave, and bore your girlfriends into a coma.

A quick aside here. It is perfectly acceptable to bore your girlfriends to death at the following times:

1. When you first meet someone.
2. When you break up with your fella.

You are allowed to bore them as in the past they have bored you. This is a well-known part of the *Girlfriend Pact*. What is not acceptable and what is definitely not part of the *Girlfriend Pact* is indiscriminate, long-term, mid-relationship boring. Keep up this carry-on and you'll find yourself sans girlfriends, and then you'll be stuck in that relationship forever because you'll have no one to complain to should it ever break up.

Nervous much?

Dating and meeting new people in general is no picnic. Unless you are a career politician you're going to feel apprehensive. So far so normal. You don't however want to get to a point where you are crippled with the jitters.

At some point before your date you need to write down your assets. Come on, babe, what are your good points? No, I'm not talking about your legs or your lips, but you. What makes you who you are. Are you kind? Generous? Loyal? Practical? Funny?

It's far too easy to be a critic, especially when it comes to ourselves. Most of us have an internal running commentary telling us why we can't, why we shouldn't and consistently, persistently reminding us of how terrible we are at everything.

About now that voice is blocking out things for your pro-list. It's telling you all the bad things you think about yourself, reminding you of all the times you screwed up and generally making you feel a bit crap. It's hard to build self-esteem and to maintain it when you have a crabby internal voice constantly undermining you. We say things to ourselves in our own head that we would never, ever, say to another person. We make pronouncements about ourselves that we would be outraged to hear anyone else say about our friends and family.

How can a girl be expected to get through a date, never mind enjoy it, with a chorus of disapproval going on her head? Anyway, it's impossible to make conversation with someone if you can't hear them above the din. (See *Silencing Your Inner Carmel* on how to deal with self-generated negativity.)

It's Not Just A River in Egypt

All of us deal with our anxieties in different ways. Some of us withdraw and isolate. Then there's the other crew that overcompensate by acting arrogantly and always, always being right. The main thing is to try for balance. However, in order to be balanced you have to actually know what you are feeling, to acknowledge feeling hurt or rejected or just plain lousy.

Now I'm sorry but I'm going to have to use the D word. Yep. *Denial.*

Denial, in itself is not a bad thing. Like all the other little tricks our brain has devised for us, sometimes we need a dose of denial in order to function and get through difficult situations. Long-term use of the D word is where it all goes a bit pear-shaped. If you continuously deny your feelings instead of experiencing them, the end result is not pretty. Long-term avoidance of dealing with your feelings will have a negative impact on your physical and mental health.

Why deny your feelings? Could it be that you are ashamed of them? Wanting to experience love isn't something bad. It's normal and it's human. Being ashamed of wanting to be loved is as silly as being ashamed of being hungry, or of wanting a big coat on a cold day. These are all human desires. They're hardwired into our physical and emotional make-up. Having guilt or shame about wanting someone to love and to love you back is like a dog being embarrassed about barking.

Here's another thing about dogs. You won't find the average dog sitting in its kennel thinking to itself. "I *shouldn't* have barked at the postman this morning." "I *must* wag my tail more." "I *should* get up earlier and run around the garden more often during the day." "I swore blind that I was going to cut back on the salivating and panting and here I am at it again. What a bad dog I am, what a bad useless terrible dog."

As far as anyone knows, dogs don't set hard standards for themselves and then kill themselves with guilt about not being able to live up to them. Now I know people are a little bit more complex than dogs but take a leaf from Fido's book and stop setting yourself up for a fall.

Feng Shui For The Soul

I know a lot of people and maybe you're one of them, who think Feng Shui is a load of old cobblers. Whether or not you buy into it, a lot of the 'practice' of Feng Shui is just sense dressed up in a kimono. One of the things most Feng Shui books will tell you is to clear out your closets and wardrobes to help unblock the energies of your household. Eh? What? My Mum put it a lot better, 'clear out the old to make way for the new'. Time to clear out all of that negativity and move on.

A Field Guide to the Irish Male

Bragman

How to Spot Him:

Within three minutes of meeting Bragman you will know what 'wheels' he drives, the mileage of said wheels, how many flat-screen tellies he owns, how big his house is, how big his salary is and how big his head is (bigger than all of the rest of it put together).

Habitat:

Cigar bars, private clubs, black-tie balls and civic receptions.

What he says:

"Top of the range." This describes everything he owns and himself. "This cost me a packet, but you pay for quality, don't you."

What you'll never hear him say:

"Labels are for losers."

Chapter Thirteen

The 'C' Word

Changed, changed utterly: a fabulous beauty is born

So you've been doing all of this work on yourself, exercising, eating properly, cutting back on the negativity and fast food, and making lists to beat the band. What's next?

Sorry but now it's time for the C word.

CHANGE

Whatever you've been doing up until now it's obviously not working. If it was, you wouldn't be reading this book. So it's time to put some other changes into motion.

The certainty of misery or the misery of uncertainty?

Your choice, babe. Which is it to be? Nobody likes change. Some eejits pretend they do, but they don't. Change is not universally popular but that doesn't mean it's necessarily a bad thing. It's an ill wind that blows no good, right?

Change = Opportunity

A fabulous beauty is born

Sometimes change – moving beyond your comfort zone is forced upon you – losing your job or a loved one; moving to a new area; divorce. When change is enforced you have no option but to adapt. What's harder in many ways is to make changes yourself. It's so easy to slip into a routine, a rut. It's comfortable, it's familiar but then again so are those smelly slippers you've been wearing since 2001. Because something is familiar doesn't mean it's good. It's time to buy yourself some new slippers, babe.

Ditching the Habit

You can't expect to effect a change overnight. Moaning and complaining, like other bad habits, have been acquired over time and are hard to ditch cold turkey. Force yourself to think or say something positive every day. I know you might be thinking, 'Oh yeah, if you had my life, you'd know there wasn't much to smile about'. You know what? That's utter tripe.

So you didn't win the lotto, big bloody deal. Is the sun shining today? Did it shine for even ten minutes? Did the bus actually come on time? Did you get a seat? Did the boss call in sick? These are just small examples.

Instead of focusing on everything that's wrong in your life, make a gratitude list. Write down all the things you are grateful for.

No ideas? Nothing to be grateful for? OK then here's mine.

1. I love my Mum and she loves me.
2. I have the most wonderful friends in the world.
3. Dogs. All dogs, even the fecker that bit me when I was a toddler.

4. Walking by the sea in all weathers.

5. Flowers. I haven't a clue what most of them are called but I love looking at them.

6. Having the opportunity to shake hands with Bill Clinton. (I would have been a hell of a lot more grateful if it had been a bit more than a handshake but let's not quibble.)

7. Having Lasik surgery three years ago and being able to see things in the distance without having to wear fecky glasses or fiddly contact lens.

8. Being able to read. I would go mad without books and magazines. Maaaaad, I tell you.

9. Getting a great deal on my laptop.

10. Having the use of all of my limbs.

I could go on. See there are plenty of things we can be happy about. I forgot to add my bed to that list. I probably am more grateful for my bed than I am for flowers if the truth be told. Not only do I have a lovely bed, but I have a roof over it. You see where I'm going with this, right?

One other thing about my list, did you notice that only two items, the Lasik surgery and my laptop, can have a monetary value placed on them.

Now it's your turn. Make your list.

1

2

3

4

5

6

7

8

9

10

Now that you've done that, try to do something every day that makes you feel good about yourself, or at the very least a little bit better about yourself. It doesn't have to be earth-shattering: nobody is asking you to find a cure for AIDS or win a Nobel Peace Prize. But hey, if you think you know the solution to world hunger, how to end senseless warfare and have an antidote to the AIDS virus, don't let me stop you.

All By Myself

My Mum likes to say, "This is the performance, *not* the dress rehearsal." In other words, you get only one chance at this life, so you may as well live it. Give yourself a goal of having one brand-new experience every week. Now this doesn't have to be a huge grand earth-shattering event every seven days.

Go out for a meal alone.

Yes, dine alone. You wouldn't believe the amount of girls I've met who think the worst thing that could befall them is having to have a meal by themselves. In this day and age. War, famine, contagious diseases, sexually transmitted diseases, Bush getting in for a second term, another series of *The Lyrics*

Board and they think the WORST thing that could happen is having a meal by themselves.

Dining alone does not, as some would have you believe, announce you as a LOSER to the entire world. For example, when you go on a business trip you have no choice in the matter. A few years back I was on a business trip to Washington D.C. I asked this lovely man if he knew of anywhere nice I could go for dinner. He said he knew plenty of lovely places and would I mind if he joined me. Not at all, said I and yadda yadda yadda, suddenly I was volunteering for every single trip to the nation's capital. Not only did I land myself a lovely boyfriend, but I got a promotion into the bargain.

If you don't fancy having an entire meal by yourself then make a point of going for coffee, ON YOUR OWN. Feel free to bring a book or a magazine to take the bare look off yourself. DO NOT and I repeat DO NOT spend your meal time blathering away on your mobile. For starters you are making yourself unapproachable and secondly the other diners will think you're an obnoxious yokel.

If you still find the idea of eating by yourself in public horrifying, then pretend that you're a high-flying executive on a business trip. You may as well, like I said before. There's no tax on thinking and other people are not able to read your thoughts. Just as well. I'd have been locked up years ago.

If you can learn to be by yourself and be comfortable by and with yourself, then it follows that you'll be comfortable with other people. It won't eliminate nerves on a first date, but it will certainly ensure that they don't take over and ruin your night. I'm not advocating that you forsake society and enter an enclosed order or go and live in a shack in the woods in Montana. Some of us, for various reasons, cannot bear to be on our own.

Spending time by yourself outside of the home has two functions:

1. It gives you time and space to think about who you are and what you want. If you don't have a clue about the first part then you have no chance with the second part. Being by yourself even for short periods of time gives you the opportunity to stop defining yourself by your relationship to others. Apart from being someone's sister/daughter/mother/ teacher/ boss, who are you?

2. Getting out and about will broaden your horizons, make you a far more interesting person (to yourself and others) and you will increase your chances of meeting someone by 100%, than if you were sitting home watching *Fair City*.

Being happy with yourself and your own company is not only a valuable life tool but also an invaluable dating one. If you are content with yourself then if and when a man comes along he will not be the repository of all of your hopes and dreams. Dear God in heaven, the pressure. The disappointment. A man, any man, being the be-all and end-all of your existence is a passport to sure-fire disappointment. Placing this amount of responsibility for your wellbeing on another individual makes you very needy. Needy is a close relative of desperate and is about as attractive as the forgotten take-away at the back of the fridge.

Self Esteem At No Cost

How do you knock your self-esteem into shape? Well, the good news is you don't need thousands of euros because it's not something you can buy. The even better news is that it's not actually all that hard to build up either. One of the easiest, quickest ways to boost flagging self-esteem is by performing an 'estimable act' i.e. one which increases your self-worth. This does not have to be a big deal, in fact most estimable acts are small and simple. Here are some suggestions.

1. Make your bed in the morning before you leave the house. Yes, I'm aware of how crazy things are in the morning; nobody has time to do diddley. Seriously, how long does it take to shake out the duvet and reposition the pillows? Coming home to a made bed is lovely. It makes a good day better and won't make a bad one worse.

2. Offer your seat on the bus to an old/pregnant/disabled person. They deserve the seat a hell of a lot more than you do, and it's good karma.

3. Pick up litter on the street, and more importantly don't discard your own litter willy-nilly.

4. Wear nice knickers. So who cares if no one else gets to see them? You are doing this for yourself.

5. Buy some lovely sheets for your bed. Isn't it a fabulous feeling when you get between freshly laundered sheets after a hard day?

6. Stock up on lovely shower gel and body lotion and then USE IT – you are worth it.

123

7. Prepare a lovely meal for yourself and eat it at the table with proper cutlery and a linen napkin.

8. Splurge on an expensive perfume and wear it every day. (Aggregate out the cost over the long time the fragrance will last and it's a bargain!)

9. When your parents start giving you unsolicited advice about your career/love life/domestic abilities – let them. Yes, bite your tongue. Nobody's saying you have to heed their advice and they'll be thrilled they've had their say.

10. Smile at someone. Make *their* day.

A Field Guide to the Irish Male

The Enabler

How to Spot Him:

The Enabler comes in many shapes and forms, traditional nerd (skinny and short-sighted) to bona fide Fine Thing (strapping and handsome). The thing that distinguishes the Enabler from other boys is that he will agree with everything you say. No matter how wrong or self-destructive your behaviour, the Enabler will always back you up. He'll support you no matter what. The meaner you are to him the more he will love you for it.

Habitat:

Waiting anxiously – in hospital waiting rooms, by the phone so he can drive fifty miles in a shower of hailstones to pick you up, outside the pub (because that's where you told him to wait), St. John of God's on visiting day.

What he says:

"Yes, anything you say." "Of course." "How high?"

What you'll never hear him say:

"No."

Chapter Fourteen

Ever-expanding Circles

Running rings around the boys

Here, There and Everywhere

Out There is a scary place. Some people think *Out There* is bars and nightclubs. It is, but as you can see from *Location, Location, Location* it's just about everywhere else too. Now, babe, apart from signing up for sailing lessons and on-line dating, another good way to meet a boy is in expanding your social network. Not only will this increase your chances of meeting someone nice but it will also keep the dreaded desperation at bay.

Prince Charming is very unlikely to come rolling up to your house on a big white charger and ask you where you've been all his life. Yes, I'm sure there are girls who've gotten off with the window cleaner, the gardener or the cable man but seriously how often do you think that happens? For that matter, how many girls do you know with gardeners?

1. Go to a lecture on something you find interesting, or even something you know absolutely nothing about.

2. Go for a walk.

3. Go for a coffee in a café you've never visited before.

On the other hand you could try frequenting a local coffee shop on a regular basis. In no time at all you'll be on first-name terms with the staff and the other regulars. My friend Patrick has worked in bars and restaurants for over twenty years. He has several LTF's (Long Term Friends) who were originally customers in an establishment where he worked. He's also had plenty of intimate encounters with people he met in the same way.

Knowing the staff and other regulars in the local coffee shop is also handy when you're dying for a caffeine fix and you can't find your cash card, or indeed when you need to find a carpenter or locksmith in a hurry.

Network News

Tell people that you are looking for a boyfriend. Now I know exactly what you're thinking – "This is going to make me look completely desperate." Well, that's where you're wrong, babe. It's all in the delivery.

"If I don't find a boyfriend soon I'm going to die."

Now there's a statement which makes you sound desperate all right.

"I'm between boyfriends at the minute and open to suggestions."

127

What does that say? It says you are a woman in charge of her own destiny. It marks you out as a confident woman who is not afraid to ask for what she wants.

A lot of people don't 'own up' to being on the lookout for a potential partner because they're ashamed. Irish people have some cracked ideas about romance, and the notion that actively wanting to connect physically and emotionally with a member of the opposite sex is somehow shameful is right at the top of the list.

Let's return briefly to the car/job metaphor. When you're looking for a new car or a new job you don't keep it a secret. You ask around knowing that this will increase your chances of landing a good job or getting a better deal on a motor. You're not at all ashamed of wanting a good car at the best possible price so why on earth feel dodgy about actively looking for a relationship? Ditch any of those lingering feelings of shame and embarrassment; apart from everything else, they're so last century.

Toxic Friends

Some Friends Are Better Than Others

Most people when they hear you are on the look-out for a new fella will be supportive. They'll keep an eye out at work, at family gatherings, down the pub and amongst their boyfriend's single friends. They'll tell you when they think someone is a good prospect and worth pursuing and they'll also tell you when they think a man is pure trouble and to get rid ASAP. They will do all of these things because they are your friends.

Mostly your friends are your friends for good reason. You like them, they like you and that's that. You have common interests, a shared history and you look out for each other. Unfortunately this is not a universal truth. Many years ago I knew a girl who was a bit on the heavy side. We'll call her Olivia. She always took great care with her hair and her make-up but despite doing her best she didn't have the greatest of luck pulling. She hung out with another girl who was noticeably skinnier than her. Let's call her Gail. When they went out together, Gail was usually the one to get lucky. One night the two girls were in a bar and a fella started to chat one of them up. However, things weren't going according to the script, instead of chatting up the skinny girl our hero was making the moves on her stouter friend. When he asked Olivia what she did for a living, her so-called friend Gail immediately responded, 'She's a prostitute.' She then added a few other choice remarks, all to Olivia's detriment, and the fella suitably turned off left them to it.

Gail was never particularly nice to or about Olivia and if you spent any time at all in their company you'd begin to wonder why on earth they hung out together. Not for very nice reasons as it happens. Gail though skinnier than Olivia hadn't the type of figure that would keep Elle McPherson awake at night worrying about being scuppered for swim suit catalogues and the like. Nor was Gail particularly pretty or intelligent or as you've gathered all that pleasant. She hung around with Olivia because she felt that when men made comparisons between them she would look the better bet.

Olivia let her size dictate every decision she made in life, or rather the ones she didn't make. Olivia kept deferring decisions until she had lost weight – something that never happened. She wouldn't look for a new job until she was skinnier – 'nobody wants to hire a fat girl'; she refused to even attempt to find a proper BF (as opposed to some stray shag in the night) because, you've guessed it, 'nobody wants to go out with a fat girl.'. Poor Olivia was deeply insecure and hung on to Gail because she didn't think she deserved better treatment from a friend and why would she when fat girls don't deserve anything at all apparently.

Pity The Buzz Wreckers

It's not always easy to spot a toxic friend, especially if your self-esteem is missing in action. About ten years ago I wasn't doing all that well – in any respect. I had made a number of bad choices in life and was stuck in a dead-end job and a dead-end relationship. I had a number of friends and would not have singled out any as being particularly toxic. Then I began to get my act together and make changes. My friends all supported me and encouraged me except for one.

This particular girl resented every single successful move I made. Instead of being happy for me, she was threatened. As long as I remained unsuccessful and unhappy, she could compare herself with me and come out favourably. Toxic friends are not necessarily bad people. Generally they are deeply insecure about themselves and have zero self-esteem. Instead of doing something positive to enhance their own self-image they find someone who in their mind (and remember it's in *their* mind) is worse off than they are.

Putting Down the Put-downs

Now it's time to get brutal. Self-help is exactly that. Help yourself and ditch the toxic friends. When you are in a position to cope with their insecurity, fine, go ahead and try to help them but in the meantime steer clear. Friends are people who care for you and love you, not people who bask in your insecurity and celebrate your failures.

These people are easy to spot if you know what to look for. They are masters of the casual put-down. They will ensure your failure before you even try.

"What would you know about that?"

"Go ahead, if you want to make a complete fool out of yourself."

People like this are basically parasites who prey on your insecurities. Worse, they are buzz wreckers. Show them the door.

I know well that you are probably too nice to be that brutal but it's no excuse for failing to stand up for yourself. If someone is always putting you down then don't just bow your head and take it meekly. *Answer back.* Seriously, who died and made them God?

"What would you know about that?" the buzz-wrecking 'friend' states.
"Nothing," you reply, "but I intend to find out."
"Go ahead if you want to make a complete fool out of yourself," the toxic friend sneers.
"So what if I do?" you reply. "So I make a fool out of myself, big bloody deal."

At this point the toxic friend will either become defensive or else back away. The latter is usually done in the following way.

"Jays, relax the head will ya? I was only slagging."

What A Slag

"I was only slagging." These are great words to hide behind. Nobody wants to be called a dry gobshite for not being able to take a slagging. You know damn well when someone is slagging you in good fun and when they aren't. CALL THEM ON IT.

Toxic friends are in essence bullies; they are using words instead of their fists. Your toxic friend will never give your needs priority. She doesn't want you to meet a fella and be happy, because then there's a danger that you won't be at her beck and call.

Why waste your time with these dreadful people when you have other lovely friends who genuinely want what's best for you? Friends who are prepared to set you up on blind dates.

Set-ups and Blind Dates

This is where you really need an open mind. Getting a friend to set you up is a risky business, but trying to meet someone new is all about risk. And come on, babe, it's not as bad as tying a big elastic around your waist and jumping off a bridge. Right.

Last year Sinead's husband set me up on a blind date. The important words in that last sentence were 'set me up'. The man in question was described as 'rich and handsome'. What's not to like? Trust me, plenty. The chap was not at all handsome, he wasn't anywhere in the neighbourhood of handsome, he was actually on another planet millions and millions of light years away from handsome. Never let it be said that I don't take my own advice. I didn't immediately discount him on the basis of his looks, or lack thereof. No, it wasn't his physical appearance that marked his card; it was the rest of it.

He may very well have been rich. A lot of rich people stay that way by refusing to put their hand in their pockets to pay for anything and he was among their number. He was so tight he'd give the average *Captain Tightfist* a run for his (closely guarded) money.

Worse again, he was a snob, a pompous arrogant condescending intellectual snob. He spent the entire date lecturing me on Russian literature and why it was better than any other in the known universe. If I hadn't been so annoyed I'd have fallen asleep with boredom.

In short, the set-up was a complete disaster. However, it was an hour and a half out of my life and I got hours and hours of fun recounting the date from hell to my girlfriends. I took a risk, and although it didn't pay off in the way I expected – meeting a lovely rich and handsome man, it paid off in other ways – giving my friends and me a good laugh.

Emma also suffered through a very memorable blind date. A friend of hers in the fashion business set her up with a guy she knew in the industry. In retrospect the fact that the boy in question was 'something in fashion' should have been clue enough as to what was to follow.

Emma's friend described her date as very good-looking. "I spotted him the minute he walked in the door," Emma said. "He was definitely the best-looking person in the place, the most beautiful in fact." Emma's date was kitted out in the very latest fashion, 'a lovely little tank top and a pair of matching trews'.

Warning bells began to clang as soon as her date sat down. The very first thing that Emma noticed was that his eyebrows were even more perfectly plucked and styled than her own. If that wasn't enough his conversation was camper than a boy scout troupe decorating a Christmas tree. Every sentence was sprinkled with "Oh, Puh-leeze" a-plenty, along with lots of eye-rolling and head-tossing, lip-pursing and gesticulation. Then he let drop the fact that people were always accusing him of being gay. Emma seizing the opportunity said, "And what do you say to them?"

"Oh, Puh-leeze!" Eye-roll. Head-toss. Lip-purse. Hand in the air. "I tell them, the first thing I think about in the morning is a woman's torso!"

Right. For the record, the first thing I think about in the morning is generally, "COFFEE. I want coffee," and then in rapid succession, "Christ, is that the time?" By the by, don't you find the expression 'a woman's torso' rather suspect? In general if you hear a man use the expression 'a woman's torso' and he's not

A. A doctor/surgeon/pathologist
B. An artist

run! Run as fast as your strappy high heels will let you. The chances are that if he's not a serial killer he's seriously deranged and to be avoided at all costs. Emma didn't linger long after the woman's torso disclosure, which is probably why she's still around to tell the yarn today.

If you are being set up on a blind date, then keep it relatively short. Meet for coffee or for a stroll around a gallery. That way if it is a disaster or you are simply not clicking then at least you won't waste too much of your precious leisure time.

If it is a disaster like the dates Emma and I had, notch it up to experience. If it is a case of simply not clicking, offer to introduce the guy to other single women that you know. The chances are he will have some single friends and want to reciprocate the offer. Hey, you never know.

Pack It In

Hunting in packs might seem like a good idea but it isn't. Few men are brave enough to run the gauntlet of a whole swarm of women on the pull. Who can blame them? Would you want to approach a boy if he was surrounded by fifteen of his closest friends? Didn't think so.

No matter how threatening a big group of boys may be, they're nothing compared to a swarm of women. It would take an extremely brave man (or a complete lunatic) to even attempt to chat up a girl who is part of a large group of females. If a man does approach you under these circumstances and he's not drunk out of his mind or a loony, then he is a very brave man indeed and definitely worthy of further consideration.

A Field Guide to the Irish Male

Closet Boy

How to Spot Him:

He is exquisitely dressed and his eyebrows are better plucked than yours. He goes to the gym about ten times a week, has the body of a god and it ain't Buddha.

Habitat:

The gym, rugby matches, seminaries and Pet Shop Boys concerts.

What he says:

"I am completely heterosexual. I love women, I mean really. I love having sex with women, millions of women. I can't have enough sex with enough women, seriously."

What you'll never hear him say:

"I'm gay."

Chapter Fifteen

Boy Ploys

When there is a point to pretence and posing, and when there isn't

Self-Conscious Objector?

Fear of rejection is at the heart of self-consciousness. Look, there's no pretty way of saying this: if you're looking for a relationship, rejection is an inevitable part of the process.

The next time you are in the cinema take a good long look at Colin Farrell, or Nicole Kidman, or anyone else for that matter whose name appears on the credits at the end. Seriously look at every name on the credits from the star to the guy with one line.

Done that?

OK. How did they get there? How did those names get on to the credit roll? Did a fairy turn up at Colin Farrell's christening waving her magic wand and saying, 'He shall be a huge success in de filums'? Did Nicole Kidman enter a pact with Satan (and I'm not talking about her marriage to Tom Cruise, by the way)? It's doubtful, right?

Do you for a second imagine that Al Pacino got cast in every part he auditioned for?

If Nicole Kidman had given up acting after her first rejection, would there be an Oscar on her mantelpiece today?

Rejection is horrible. There are no two ways about it. It's one of the most horrible things a person can experience. But it happens. And guess what, IT WON'T KILL YOU.

Silly Schemes

Plenty of publications will give you strategies and tactics to avoid being rejected by the man you want. Not this one. It's like your Internet picture or pretending to like dogs. The truth will catch up with you in the end.

Adopting poses and playing games is exhausting and ultimately counter-productive. Unless you are willing to keep up the pretence forever. What's the point? If you are pretending to be someone you are not, then you are *not* the woman of his dreams and one of these fine days he's going to wake up, realise he's been duped and won't be very happy about it. Where does that leave you? Exactly.

Olivia met John when she was on holiday in Greece. As he lived in another part of the country, their first 'date' back home was an all-weekend affair. Olivia felt very insecure about the fact that John had gone to university and she hadn't. Before he arrived at her flat she borrowed 'intellectual' books from her flatmate to display prominently around her bedroom. John was really excited to see that he and Olivia had the same taste in books and wanted to discuss them in detail. Of course, Olivia hadn't read any of the books, so you can imagine what a great start the weekend got off to.

Poor Olivia, if only she'd had enough confidence in herself to see that John liked her for who she was. He wouldn't have made such a big effort to see her again after the holiday was over if he wasn't interested. On the reverse side, remember if you are going to lie about yourself, your book and CD collection (or lack of one) will speak volumes about you – so be careful.

To be fair, the image you present on a date and when on the pull is not who you actually are. Everyone knows this. You know it, the boy knows it and casual passers-by know it. This persona is usually a souped-up version of yourself. It's your better self, your nicer, funnier, more patient and caring self. In a nutshell it's your *Stepford Wife* self. You are charming, funny, fragrant, caring, patient, loving and always wearing fancy underwear.

Inevitably real life starts to reassert itself and patience wears thin. When the honeymoon period ends you will not always have perfectly glossy hair, you won't be fascinated by a detailed account of what went on in the rugby club on Thursday night and your less fancy knickers will see the light of day again. All perfectly normal so far.

However, and this is the big but, the person that emerges at the end of the honeymoon period should bear at least some resemblance to the person he started going out with. You know, someone who shares the same qualities as the glowing goddess he first met, even if you do occasionally have greasy hair, PMS or hairy legs. If you've been faking it all, you *will* come a cropper. That's an iron-clad guarantee.

Sensible Strategy

Having said that, there are some tactics that don't involve pretending to be something you ain't.

Say you're attending a lecture/evening class/business symposium. Don't just run in and sit anywhere. No, stop and take a good look around. Is there anybody you particularly would like to sit beside? Then go sit there.

This is vitally important if the event in question is the first in a series. Most of us tend to be creatures of habit and unconsciously repeat patterns. Be careful where you sit on week one and whom you sit beside because you might be stuck there every following week.

If this is a one-off deal then fine, you'll have to put chat on him there and then. Easier said than done? Not at all. Just ask him if he knows what time it is. Don't try this one if there's a bloody big clock on the wall facing you. "Have you taken this class before?" is a good one.

Ice-Breakers or Pickaxes?

Believe it or not, speech is actually a hindrance to proper communication, especially when you're trying desperately to make a good impression on someone and your tongue is

141

tied up like a Tory politician in a House of Domination. Unfortunately, if you fancy someone you're going to have to talk to them eventually.

Hands up who hasn't heard a million cheesy chat-up lines? I polled a number of women and asked them to tell me the worst chat-up lines they'd ever heard.

And now without any further ado, the Worst Chat-Up Line Ever is

"Do you have any Irish in you? Want some?"

Luckily not all chat-up lines are as gross as that. For sheer cheesetasticness take a look at the following

"Did it hurt? When you fell from heaven?"

"I lost my phone number. Can I have yours." (I quite like this one myself).

"Do you believe in love at first sight or should I walk by again?" (I happen to like this one as well; I guess cheesy works for me!)

"Be unique and different, say yes to me."

"Your feet must hurt because you've been running through my head all day long." (Too cheesy even for me.)

My friend Jeannie remembers the half-beer mat approach which gained popularity when it featured on a television advert for a particular German beer. "At one point in Dublin you couldn't go out for the night without some drunken fool approaching you and giving you half a soggy beer mat, then he'd hold up the other half wink and say something very unfunny like

> *"Hong Kong next Tuesday. Oh, shite, I can't make it. How about my place tonight?"*

I thought that line was quite funny. "Not," Jeannie said, "when you hear it repeated constantly by gobshites who couldn't spell Hong Kong let alone go there." Fair enough.

And then there's the plain lame

> *"Don't I know you from somewhere?"*

> *"I lost my keys and have nowhere to stay."*

And the really really stupid

> *"You know you could be a model if you lost some weight."*

And finally the uber-romantic

> *"How would you like to be buried with my people?"*

A Field Guide to the Irish Male

Drama King

How to Spot Him:

Easy. You'll probably hear him before you see him. The only thing he likes better than having a meltdown is doing it in front of an audience. If the Drama King wants to confront you about something he'll wait until you're in a crowded restaurant or bar, all the better to make a dramatic exit when he's done shouting.

Habitat:

He's often found in front of you in the supermarket queue, giving out yards to the checkout girl, usually when you're in a big hurry. Court ordered anger management courses.

What he says:

"Shut up and listen to me." "You NEVER listen to me."

What you'll never hear him say:

"Let's discuss this rationally." "I'm sorry I was wrong."

Chapter Sixteen

Great Expectations

If you want God to laugh – tell Him your plans

Expectations: Disappointments under construction

Expectations, great or small, are the first step on the path to being gutted. A boy you fancy rings you and asks you out. He's a bit of a ride and seems to be in full possession of his faculties so you accept. However, before you've even put the receiver down your head is buzzing. THIS IS IT. He's the one. By the time you actually meet up for dinner/drinks/a coffee, you've already mapped out the entire course of the relationship in your head. You've taken mental pictures of your wedding and named the children. OK, that might be a bit extreme, (but I know girls who've done it; to be fair I've done it myself). What happens when things fail to go as planned – when he doesn't drop to one knee and propose during the dessert course or over the frappucino? Major disappointment, that's what.

The key with any date and/or relationship is

ACCEPT *don't* **EXPECT**

In other words, it is what it is, and take it for that. No amount of fantasising on your part will change the reality. He's either into you or he isn't. He'll want to see you again or he won't. A relationship may or may not develop. It will work or it won't.

Do remember as well that when you build up someone in your head, that image has nothing to do with them. When they go and act like themselves, it will again lead to disillusion, disappointment and despair.

Everyone does this at some point. I once went out with a lad, let's call him Jim, who had all of the external stuff. He was pretty good–looking, had a fabulous flat and drove a car that made other boys drool with envy. Don't ask me the make, all I know is that it was German and whenever we left it parked we would invariably come back to find another boy stroking it lovingly. The other boy would look at Jim with a mixture of awe and envy and Jim would look smug.

Everything looked so good on paper that I cheerfully ignored the fact that Jim was a pompous windbag who thought a great deal too much of himself and very little about others. Jim's opinion was the only one that mattered but that was OK because Jim was an expert on EVERYTHING. Name a subject, any subject, and Jim could expound on it at length, at very great length indeed. Jim was the type of man who would, and did, order for the entire table at a restaurant. He would belittle other people for their beliefs. Feng Shui – a load of shite. Vegetarians – a bunch of cranks. I never got to meet his Mammy but I have a funny feeling that she waited on him hand and foot, and HE LET HER.

147

Like anyone who's in denial I just kept ignoring the things that didn't fit in with the lovely mental image I had constructed. However, Jim was so tiresome that eventually even my denial grew weary of him and slunk off before it got bored to death. Mind you, I still look back on his lovely flat with great fondness. It was after all, his best feature.

The problem with scenarios like this one is that you are setting yourself up for a big let-down. The chap doesn't know the script in your head. He doesn't even know he's in a play. He hasn't a clue that there's a plot he's supposed to be following, lines he's supposed to say, cues he's supposed to hear, entrances and exits he's supposed to make. He thought he was just having a casual drink or bite to eat and he's innocently going about the business of being himself. Eventually he'll behave in character (his own, not the fictional one you've ascribed to him) and you won't be able to ignore it. You'll be angry and disappointed and meanwhile, he's got no clue why.

See, here's the thing, the BIG SECRET,
– men are people too.

Men are not inanimate objects that we can neatly fit into our lives and then utilise as we see fit. This is why most sensible women prefer shoes to men.

Why Most Women Prefer Shoes To Men

Shoes are reliable.
Shoes compliment and flatter us.
Shoes are unlikely to run off on another pair of feet.

True, but don't you have a couple of neglected pairs lying at the bottom of the wardrobe? Remember how it started out.

There was such promise. You saw them and instantly fell in love. You knew before you even tried them on that these shoes were the ONES. They were the shoes you'd been looking for your entire life. They were more than you could afford but you couldn't live without them. It was destiny; you were meant to be together.

The first time you put them on they weren't actually all that comfy. You persevered, you thought you could change them, break them in, and mould them to your will. And where are those shoes now? That's right! At the bottom of the wardrobe and every time you see them you begrudge the fortune you paid for them.

What applies to shoes applies to men. If the fit isn't right at the start, no amount of suffering is going to make it any better. The great thing about shoes is that you can never have too many on the go at the one time. They're a lot easier to handle than men in that regard.

Happily Ever After . . .

You had fantasies about those shoes, didn't you? It's not unusual to indulge in the odd fantasy or two about the man you fancy. Do keep in mind they are fantasies. They are in your head. Reality is a separate place. Don't fall into the *Curse of Wishful Thinking*. Don't ignore the early warning signs. They're there for a reason. It's far easier to walk away from someone who's not suitable before you've invested time in the relationship and also, before you've slept with them.

Most of us grew up with fairy tales which began 'Once upon a time' and ended with 'and they all lived happily ever after'. For many of us this was our first brush with male/ female relationships. And janey did it ever set us up for disappointment. In *Cinderella*, *Snow White*, *Rapunzel* and *Sleeping Beauty* the heroines passively wait for the handsome prince to gallop by and rescue them from their quite miserable lives. Out of all of them Cinderella is the only one to actually leave the house and only then because her fairy godmother makes her. The other lassies just hang around the house waiting, waiting, waiting.

Plenty of us non-fairytale-heroine girls are equally passive when it comes to our own romantic lives. We're given the impression early on that our romantic lives are fated, the perfect mate will just turn up out of the blue and off we'll head into the sunset. Would any of us be this lax about the rest of our lives? Would you sit at home waiting for your ideal job to come knocking on the door. Hardly, you'll be actively sending out CVs and poring over the newspaper. If you want a new outfit you don't wish on moonbeams and stars; you get your ass down to the shops and buy one. When you're purchasing a car you don't just settle for the first thing with four wheels and a steering wheel that you come across. Not on your nellie. You'll have a plan, you'll know where to look and more importantly what you're looking for. You'll have thought well in advance about the model, the size, the colour and what you can afford. What you do not do is leave your potential vehicle, something which is a long-term investment, to chance. You certainly don't expect a fairy godmother to appear in a haze of twinkling lights and turn a handy pumpkin into a Ferrari.

Groundhog Man

Have you found yourself in the same crappy relationship

time and time again? Has your dating life been a case of same excrement, different flies? If it has, then don't for a second think you're unique. Plenty of us have been there, done him. If you're constantly being let-down by fellas or every encounter/relationship/coupling is a case of déjà vu all over again, then you need to ask yourself why.

Is there a pattern? Do you always end up with losers/ cheaters/louts/cheapskates/all of the above? OK, what you need to do now is figure out why. There could be any number of reasons why you repeat the same unhealthy pattern time and time again. It could date back to your relationship with your own father, or lack of one. It could be that even though you think you want to be in a relationship, deep down you really are frightened of making a commitment. It could be that your self-esteem is in the toilet and you don't think you deserve to be treated properly by men. Once you know why your relationships seem to follow the same screwed-up template, then it will be a hell of a lot easier to break the pattern.

In Grainne's case the pattern was quite deliberate. She deliberately chose men she wasn't all that into. "I wanted to have the balance of power on my side so I always chose men who were mad about me but I didn't actually fancy all that much." The result was that the sexual part of the relationship usually wasn't all that great and Grainne soon grew bored. After a number of failed relationships Grainne realised that she might need to take a few emotional risks in order to have the relationship she wanted.

Saoirse is aware of her pattern and trying hard to change it. "I'm always sleeping with men on the first date," she said. "Even ones I really like and then I get upset when they don't call me. I'm trying very hard to stop doing this."

Repeating the same behaviour over and over again and expecting different results is beyond futile, it's actually quite insane. Look, if you put your hand in the fire and burned it would you continue to keep sticking your fingers in the flames expecting them not to be singed? Exactly. The first step to changing a pattern of behaviour is recognising it.

So if you've been essentially having the same relationship time and time again then it's time to stop sticking your hand in the fire.

It's time to Try Something Different.

It's time to get out there and start dating up a storm.

A Field Guide to the Irish Male

Crustie Boy

How to Spot Him:

Spotting him is hard. The person beneath the matted dreads, several layers of wool and several more layers of dirt could easily be male or female. Who can tell? Whatever a Crustie's sex they are rarely seen without their standard accessories — a large plastic bottle of industrial strength cider, a pouch of loose tobacco and rolling papers.

Habitat:

Protests, riots, Glastonbury, and sitting outside broken-down caravans surrounded by several dirty barefoot crustie babies and mangy dogs.

What he says:

"Man." "Fuck." "Spliff."

What you'll never hear him say:

"A glass of chilled chardonnay, please."

Part Four

Painting the Town

On your marks, get set and go, go, go

Chapter Seventeen

A New York State Of Mind

A taste of the Big Apple

How many T.V. shows could you name that are set in New York? Easy-peasy. *Sex and the City, Friends, Will & Grace, Law & Order* and *The Sopranos*. Those are just the ones that spring to mind immediately. There are plenty more and let's not even get started on the number of films that take place in the Big Apple. Like a lot of Irish people I grew up watching images of New York in the cinema and on the telly. Because of this I didn't need a street map when I first moved there. However, although I could find my way to the Empire State Building and Bloomingdales without having to ask for directions, I was clueless when it came to behaving like a native. More so, because I thought I knew what I was getting myself into.

New York style dating was as alien to me as Cantonese, and almost as hard to figure out. I couldn't fathom the whole idea of announcing to the world that you were *looking*. Well, that would mean that I'd have to admit to having needs, wants and desires. Like most Irish girls I'd drifted into relationships. You know how it goes; you meet a fella, have a snog and very possibly intimate relations. Often there is no contact until the next time you 'bump into him' and so it goes and six months later voilà you're in a relationship. Neither of you ever addresses the relationship or the nature of your liaison along the way. Why is this? That would mean admitting that you actually care – God forbid.

With the NY Way you get to date multiple men at the same time. You can even have intimate relations with each of them and nobody can call you a slapper. Well, they can but they'd be wrong.

Here's a quick run down of how New York Style Dating proceeds.

Date One: The chaste-kiss-on-the-cheek date
Date Two: The snog date
Date Three: The sex date

First you go on a date. If that works out you arrange for a second and all going well a third. Date three is generally accepted as the 'Sex Date'. This is not a hard-and-fast rule, more of a guideline. If you have strong moral objections to going the Full Monty, then presumably by date three your escort will know the lie of the land.

So you and your chap date for a couple of months. Both of you are still free to see other people and indeed sleep with other people, as long as you both take precautionary measures against contracting and passing on something nasty, and perhaps lethal.

After a couple of months pass you have 'the talk' and decide

A New York State Of Mind

if you're going to see each other exclusively or discontinue the relationship.

Could anything be easier?

Quantity Street

OK, so here is your mission, should you choose to accept it. Start doing things the New York way.

Because that way you can date as many men as you want at the same time. Do not limit yourself by selecting only one or two. Most of the guys you go out with will not last beyond the first encounter so the more you meet up with the better.

The chances are that initially you won't be sleeping with any of them. However, with New York Style Dating Rules there is no prohibition against you having intimate relations with more than one man at the same time. This does not qualify you for a slapper award.

I know from personal experience and from that of my friends that a lot of Irish people balk at the idea of being intimate with more than one person at the same time. Look, the bottom line is: it's up to you. Just know that you have the choice. If you are not in a committed relationship you are free to do whatever you want. The only obligation you have to the other person is to ensure their health does not suffer as a result of your liaison.

Silencing Your Inner Carmel

In order to have a successful date (and life) you need to turn off that internal monologue, or at the very least turn down the volume. Easier said than done I know. Try giving the voice a name. You could call it after that bitchy girl in school who always had something nasty to say. Or you could call it after that lazy co-worker who does nothing all day yet always manages to take credit for the work you've done. Then again you could christen it after your horrible ex who did nothing but put you down until you saw sense and dumped the useless eejit.

OK, so the voice has a name now. I call mine Carmel for reasons I can't divulge (on the grounds of not wanting to be sued). Feel free to use this name yourself; you have no idea how happy that would make me.

So you're going about your business when the voice starts up with all of the negative remarks. If this happens when you are alone then feel free to do the following out loud.

Warning: bad language alert

Shout, "Fuck off, Carmel (or whatever name you've chosen). Shut the hell up, who asked you!"

You would be amazed how well this works. Anger is often considered a negative emotion. Only if you let it be. It can be very empowering. Telling that negative voice to go to hell in no uncertain terms is more than empowering. Don't trust me on this; try it.

The other way to deal with constant self-criticism is to get out your list of assets and read it – slowly. You haven't done your list of assets yet? Well, do it now.

Writing things down is important. It makes them more real

161

don't you think? No? How many people do you know who enter into business ventures with only a verbal contract? My point exactly. Everything important gets written down and your assets are very important.

Imagine for a second that you are in advertising or P.R. These agencies are paid to present their client/product in the best possible light, whether it be by simply selling the person or the thing to the public or by damage limitation and control when something unsavoury has occurred.

Take a look at how well you've presented yourself to date. If an ad agency or P.R. firm had done the same job would you,

   A. Fire them.
   B. Withhold payment.
   C. Give them a bonus for a job well done.

So after doing all of the exercises to get your head in the right place for heading out on dates, how are the outsides doing?

A Field Guide to the Irish Male

Howard Hughes

How to Spot Him:

HH is an obsessive compulsive so when he's out and about he's not too hard to spot. He will ritually perform tasks in the same way, in the same order and heaven help the person who disrupts his routine. His desk is the cleanest in the office and all of the things on it are at precise right angles to each other. He is so neat that he makes the Mammy's Boy and Holy Joe look like they've spent the night in a skip.

Habitat:

A hermetically sealed germ-free environment. Failing that he will have an ultra-clean house with no carpets, plastic covers on the sofa and absolutely no pets or small children (germ magnets the lot of them) allowed. There is no seat on his loo as that would only encourage people to actually sit on it and the thought of that gives Howard palpitations.

What he says:

"Are you sure this fruit was washed?" "Please remove your shoes and place these plastic bags over your feet."

What you'll never hear him say:

"Ah, any ould way is fine."

Chapter Eighteen

Making Up Is Hard To Do

There's no need to put on a brave face

With date makeup, remember less is more. Too much makeup can make you look

A. Older
B. Like a clown
C. Desperate

The THIRD Greatest Lie Ever Told

Men just love to say they don't like make-up. "I prefer the natural look," is the third greatest untruth told by the average Irish male. In second place we have "Of course, it doesn't make you look fat." And at number one – "We can just hold each other". These three lies are totally dependent on circumstances. If a man is out with the lads then *all* tall tales usually have something to do with the alleged amount of pints he can swallow.

Girls always find the claim to prefer the natural look

unfathomable, as usually the chap in question is hooked up with a woman who is wearing the latest range from M.A.C. – all of it at the same time.

OK, here's the deal. Men really think that they don't like make-up. However, unless your name is Kate, Elle or Naomi, if you face out into that hostile place known as the real world without your 'face' on, the chances are that these same men will be giving the hairy eyeball to the painted-up lassies. Actually forget I just said that. Who the hell knows what Elle, Kate & Naomi look like without the benefit of professionally applied slap and airbrushing?

Abuse of Powders

Make-up is a much abused tool. Unless you're starring in a production of *The Elephant Man*, it's Halloween or you're going to a fancy dress contest, then you shouldn't be using make-up to change your appearance. Changing the appearance is the function of special effects stage make-up and it usually involves as much latex as it does greasepaint. Who has the time, money or patience for that carry-on?

The function of make-up is to enhance your natural features. A truly wonderful make-up is like a great acting performance; you don't see it. It looks natural. This is the natural look boys are so fond of. The goms think that's the way you woke up this morning, all dewy and glowy and lovely. They would be gobsmacked to find out you spent a good half-hour making yourself look so 'natural'.

Yes, half an hour. Any amount of time over that and guess what, you've got too much slap on. Leave the make-up bag at home. Unless you are going to shower mid-way through your date then you will not need to reapply anything except your lippie. Last year I was at a function where a number of the guests were flight attendants in their late teens and early twenties. All of them, boys and girls, were wearing copious amounts of fake tan topped off liberally with tonnes of foundation. If those runway lights ever got damaged, this lot could have done an equally good job guiding planes in to land.

At one point during the lunch I went to the ladies. One of the girls from this group was standing in front of a mirror applying mascara. When I came out of the toilet cubicle she was still there, still applying mascara. I washed my hands, dried them and reapplied my own lipstick and when I left she was still in front of the mirror, still applying mascara. Guess what? That's way too much mascara. That's more mascara than Boy George gets through in a month.

Apart from anything else it's pretty rude to spend ten minutes in the jacks reapplying your make-up when you're on a date.

Smells Like?

If make-up is abused, then the ill-treatment perfume receives defies definition. There are certain things you can get away with stinting on, fashion eye shadows for example. There are plenty of cheaper brands that will give you the look of the moment without any ill-effects on your eyes. Cheap and disreputable don't have to be synonymous. The same goes for a number of lipsticks, eye-liners, blushers and if you are very lucky indeed you might get away with one of the less expensive foundations.

The same, unfortunately, doesn't go for perfume. If a bottle of scent is cheap it will smell cheap, and worse, nasty. There is a direct correlation between the price of a fragrance and the amount worn. The lesser the price, the more the application. Personally I think this is an overtly offensive act. People who liberally douse themselves in cheap scent (or aftershave) are committing violence upon the rest of the community. Wearing cheap cologne is offensive; wearing huge quantities of the stuff is criminal.

Even if you have spent a lot of money on a quality brand which won't irritate the sinuses of your fellow travellers on the DART, you should still use scent sparingly. The purpose of a fragrance is to mingle with the natural smell of your body and produce a faint aroma that is uniquely you, not an overpowering whiff that could melt plastic. Remember those mysterious pheromones!

Spend wisely and use sparingly.

Forget Fashion

What you wear out is all relative and depends where your date is taking place. If he's taking you to the races or the dog track then six-inch heels and a skimpy top aren't the best choices. Forget fashion unless you are 5' 10" and weigh 6 stone. The rest of us should use glossy magazines as a guide to style *not* as a bible.

Wear what suits you. Look I know this sounds painfully obvious but make sure you are wearing the right size. There is no point in spending a fortune on a lovely outfit if it doesn't fit you properly. Ill-fitting clothes are uncomfortable, look awful and do little to increase your confidence.

What Not To Wear On A Date

1. Old undies or granny knickers – hey, you never know.

2. Any clothing belonging to your ex, T-shirt/checky shirt/ jeans etc. If for some mad reason you do wear any of these items, for goodness sake don't tell your date who they belong to. Unless you are having a crap time and want the date to end, then fire ahead.

3. Anything belonging to your mother. If you and your Mammy are sharing clothing one of you is dressing funny. (OK, maybe this doesn't apply if your mother had you when she was 16, but still…)

4. New shoes. Being crippled with blisters just ain't sexy.

5. See-through chiffon frocks. Look, unless you are J.Lo this look won't work, and to be honest I don't think it did much for her either.

Weddings, job interviews, and dates – all occasions when you obsess about what to wear. As you well know, what you wear isn't just about throwing on something and hoping for the best; it's about the overall *look*. Also, remember that unlike the person from personnel asking you where you'd like to be in five years' time (why do they still ask people this ghastly question?) your date is in with a chance of seeing you in your nudie.

When Things Start Getting A Bit Hairy

Like it or loathe it, the current fashion is for less body hair and it doesn't look like changing any time soon. Why should I bother, you say. I don't have a fella so what's the point of grooming my legs and my area? Take a tip from the boy scouts and *BE PREPARED*. You never know when you are going to meet the next big love of your life. He could be standing in the next lift you take, taking your order the next time you go out for a meal, he could at this very moment be trimming your hedges (as it were). You don't want him to have to take out the electric strimmer in the bedroom now do you?

There are several options for keeping excess body hair under control.

Waxing is probably the most common method especially for the bikini area. Luckily for wimps like me there are a few alternatives for the bikini area such as over-the-counter creams and the old fall-back of shaving. Don't attempt to do any sort of hair removal from your area on the day of a date. Even if you are not planning on taking your knickers off. Shaving and waxing can often leave you feeling raw and uncomfortable, while certain dilapatory creams leave a funny smell.

A Field Guide to the Irish Male

The Wannabees

1. Wannabe Famous

How to Spot Him:

He deliberately cultivates quirks to try to establish himself as a 'personality'. Often his clothing is so quirky that he ends up looking like a children's T.V. presenter from the 1970s, not the look he was going for.

Habitat:

Auditioning for *You're A Star* or *Big Brother*. In the cast of *You're A Star* or *Big Brother*. In the hairdresser's working on his latest wacky cut.

What he says:

"When I'm in *heat* magazine." "What has Becks got that I don't?"

What you'll never hear him say:

"Reality T.V. is useless!"

The Wannabees

2. Wannabe Gangsta

How to Spot Him:

He wears baggy pants so low-slung they are almost hanging from his ankles. He also sports a hoodie and plenty of bling. Despite the fact he's from Thurles he still speaks like he from the ghetto, know what I'm saying y'all.

Habitat:

Street corners.

What he says:

"Yo." "Whattup, G?" "Whattup, homie?"

What you'll never hear him say:

"Daniel O'Donnell is the man!"

A Field Guide to the Irish Male

The Paupers

1. The Mooch

How to Spot Him:

The Mooch is a cousin of *Captain Tightfist*. The essential difference between them is that he has no money of his own to hoard. The Mooch's wardrobe is a dead giveaway. He's been wearing the same jumper for the past six years and because charity shop clothes are haute couture for him, (he lives on hand-me-downs) he'll often be wearing clothes originally intended for girls.

Habitat:

Anywhere someone else is picking up the tab.

What he says:

"Whoops I forgot my wallet." "Are you throwing that blouse out?"

What you'll never hear him say:

"Oh no, this is my treat. I insist."

173

The Paupers

2. The Student

How to Spot Him:

Perpetually unshaven and a bit whiffy (no hot water) and usually found under a large coat (no heat). The Student is a fervent believer in The Cause – Animal Rights/The Reunification of Ireland/The Environment, The Cause itself isn't really all that important but fighting for it is. He is ultra-serious with absolutely no sense of humour. He finds it hard to consummate sexual relations as he's either too cold or has consumed too many cans of extra-strong cider on an empty stomach.

Habitat:

The college bar, anywhere there are two for one drink specials or in his 'flat' a one-room bed-sit with a communal toilet miles away down a draughty corridor. The Student will never be where he says he will be as he has no sense of time, or a watch.

What he says:

"Have you a lend of a fiver?" "Any gear?"

What you'll never hear him say:

"All drugs are evil."

Chapter Nineteen

Datiquette

First Date Etiquette

Going to the cinema on a first date is quite a good idea. If food is suggested then go after the cinema rather than before. This way if you find out you have nothing in common you will at least be able to discuss the film while having your dinner. The other way around, the trip to the cinema will become twice as tense and awkward if you've spent the previous two hours trying desperately to find something to talk about.

What's Eating You?

If you choose to dine as part of your date, think hard about what you want to eat. A first date is a very fraught occasion and can turn the most graceful of us into bumbling fools. Don't make things worse by ordering 'difficult' or messy food. You don't want to waste valuable getting-to-know-you time worrying about capturing and taming your dinner.

Foods to Avoid

Pasta and noodles that need to be wrapped around a fork, especially if they come in a heavy colourful sauce. You cannot eat these dishes daintily and will be lucky to end the night without you, him, both your respective clothing and the table cloth covered in orange splatter.

Lobster is a nightmare, all of that crushing and sucking. Fuggetaboutit. Also, it's expensive and you don't want him to think you're scabbing.

Peas. There is no winning with peas. They slither around your plate daring you to catch them, they'll fling themselves across the table given half the chance and if you do succeed in catching and eating them the chances are you'll be distinctly unfragrant later in the evening most likely about the time you're trying to have a romantic moment.

Corn on the cob. Oh dear God in heaven, the mess, the bits between the teeth, the butter running down the chin, the horror.

Garlic & Onions. Unless he's eating them too. Otherwise the kiss goodnight might be the kiss-off.

And, no more than you'd wear brand new shoes on a date, don't even think of suddenly getting adventurous and eating something you've never tried before. Unfamiliar food might not, to put it mildly, *agree* with you.

I know it sounds like stating the bloody obvious but keep your mouth closed when you are eating. There is nothing as off-putting as seeing another person's dinner being actively masticated. Actually, sorry, there is something worse: Someone talking with their mouth full and splattering your face and hair with small gobbets of food.

You'd be amazed by the number of people I've eaten with, both men and women, who thought nothing of chatting away, displaying the contents of their mouth. Yeeeuch.

There are few other habits which your dinner date might find off-putting.

DON'T eat from his plate unless he specifically offers you something. Some girls think this is the essence of feminine charm, but a lot of boys think it's really rude. They're right.

DON'T feed him from your plate. This is more than mumsy and a bit presumptuous. If you want to share your food with him, which is perfectly normal, we all like to taste what's on other people's plates, then simply cut off a piece and leave it at that.

Leave all that oochy-coochy, 'would baba like a bite?' business until much later in the relationship. By the way, if you do feel impelled to play feeding games, try to do it in the privacy of your home and not in a restaurant – it tends to put the other diners off their food.

And finally, DON'T count calories – yours or his. I once worked with a woman who was an ex-fattie. Her meal plans were as regimented as a troupe of German boy scouts and

Datiquette

she knew down to the last crumb just how many calories she was consuming. Fine, grand, good for her. However, she also counted what everybody else ate. "There's 2,500 calories in that!" she'd screech as you lifted the first forkful of food to your mouth. "That's one and a quarter times your daily allowance, and it's only lunch-time!" That was the end of enjoying your lunch.

I know full well it's not easy having to watch what you eat because I'm not one of those girls who has a super-fantastic metabolism and manages to look like a super-model on speed while stuffing her face with chocolate and pizza. I only wish. However, when I am going out for a meal, whether it is a date or just a dinner with friends, I am going out for a meal, not a poor imitation of one. I will simply have less to eat earlier in the day or do a wee bit more exercise the next day.

Nine out of ten boys who expressed a preference said they would rather see a girl with a healthy appetite. A girl who nibbles on a salad leaf (sans dressing) is rightly or wrongly considered uptight, repressed, dull and boring. Whereas a girl who displays a healthy appetite for food is generally thought to have other equally healthy appetites also.

Don't forget your mobile. The mobile phone is the greatest dating accessory ever created. The mobile has many advantages for the dating girl.

A. You don't have to give him your home/work numbers until you feel secure that he's not a stalking psychopath.

B. You don't have to wait around the house like a lemon waiting for him to call to make arrangements.

(Ask your mother what life was like for dating girls before the invention of the answering machine. If Mom won't fill you in then read a Jane Austen novel, which will give you some idea how lucky you are to be part of the mobile generation.)

C. Most importantly, the mobile gives you an 'out' clause from a date that isn't going too well. Get a friend to call you about a half-hour or so into the date. That will be plenty of time to gauge whether you want to continue with the date or would die happy knowing the datee was leaving on the next plane to take up his vocation in a Tibetan monastery. If the latter is the case you pull the requisite faces when you receive the call and then dash off pleading a family emergency. If you haven't had the sense to book your half-hour check-in call in advance, you can always text someone and get them to call you.

OK, so this isn't very nice behaviour but you're looking for a boyfriend not a canonisation. Anyway the chances are if you were having a miserable date then so was he and he'll be only too happy to see your back running out of the nearest exit.

One final note on using mobiles on dates. Keep them switched off if your date is taking place in the cinema or a theatre. A ringing mobile in the cinema is extremely anti-social. Rudeness and thoughtlessness are huge turn-offs for everyone. So is being attacked by the 20-stone biker in the row behind you, so TURN IT OFF.

Also, apart from your thirty-minute check-up call, do not

have conversations with your pals while you are on the actual date. You might think speaking to seven different people over the course of the evening makes you look really popular and desirable. In fact it makes you look like an idiot, so don't do it.

Right then, all set? Let's go.

A Field Guide to the Irish Male

The Bastards

1. The Gastronome aka The Fat Bastard

How to Spot Him:

Not as easy as you might think. Sometimes the Gastronome is so huge that you don't realise that you're looking at an actual person. He's the guy who needs a seat-belt extension and two seats on a plane.

Habitat:

Anywhere food is sold or prepared. The Gastronome pretends to be a connoisseur of fine foods but he's not above popping into Abrakebabra for a late-night snack.

What he says:

"Oh just a smidge more, please."

What you'll never hear him say:

"When."

The Bastards

2. Good-time Charlie aka The Mad Bastard

How to Spot Him:

If there's someone dancing on a table in the bar, that'll be Charlie. He's always faintly dishevelled, as if he slept in his clothes and just got out of bed (usually this is the case). He's the one urging everyone to move on to the next venue. He suffers terribly from a bad sinus condition and has a perpetual runny nose. Charlie isn't all that interested in girls (or boys). Why would he want to have sex when there are so many other ways to have fun?

Habitat:

GTC is never seen before noon. After that he can be spotted in the pub having an eye-opener. At night he wanders from pub to club to after-hours establishment. In each he spends a large amount of his time in the bathroom.

What he says:

"Whoo-hoo!" "Drink up." "Have another." "They don't call me Charlie for nothing."

What you'll never hear him say:

"I think I'll have an early night."

The Bastards

3. The Sad Bastard

How to Spot Him:

If such a thing as a Joy-o-Meter existed it would break when SB entered the room, as he sucks all joy out of the atmosphere. He's dishevelled, crumpled and always either slightly drunk or badly hung-over. But, as he says himself, if you had his problems you would be too. His wife has just run off with his best mate and/or he's just lost his job and between the crying and constant jarring-up his eyes are perpetually bloodshot.

Habitat:

Propping up the local bar at all hours of the day and night moaning to the poor barman. Other people's spare rooms.

What he says:

"Why me?" "I don't want to put you out. It's just until I get sorted."

What you'll never hear him say:

"I can't complain."

Chapter Twenty

Take Chat

Subject matters

A lot of people will advise you to avoid politics and religion when you're chatting with a stranger. Don't! This isn't a job interview. The sooner you know that the man you're chatting up is a staunch Catholic and a Fianna Fail supporter the sooner you can

A. Run like hell.

B. Jump for joy (and jump him).

C. Phone your Mammy and tell her you've found the perfect man for her.

The weather

Ah yes, the old stand-by. When there's nothing else to talk about there's always the weather. Try to avoid this route if at all possible. It marks you out as a boring sod who can't think of anything better to talk about.

The exception to this is if there's been a freak blizzard or if half the country is under four feet of water. Then it's current affairs and not the weather, so it's OK.

The other exception to the weather rule is when you can use it to demonstrate what an utterly wonderful positive person you are. "Isn't it a fabulous day? Don't you just love this weather?" Don't bitch about the current climate. Everyone does it, I know, but it's negative and, worse, boring.

Nobody likes the rain, not even, I am pretty certain, ducks. So if it's lashing rain and you have tried every other conversational gambit then fine, talk about the rain. However, don't just bitch about it; say something positive but definitely not 'it's nice weather for ducks'. There's an old Scandinavian saying along the lines of "there's no such thing as bad weather merely inadequate clothing". See, that's pretty positive.

Nothing to Say

So you think you have nothing to talk about. Nonsense. What do you find interesting? What are your obsessions?

Here's mine, in no particular order.

- Dogs
- Chocolate
- Shoes
- Handbags
- Hats
- The television shows, *Law & Order*, *Little Britain* and *Big Brother*.

- Books
- Films
- Fancy restaurants

Now if I'm in a situation where I want to bore a straight man to sobs then I'll start discussing shoes and handbags at length. If it's a straight man in whom I have no interest and he's not getting the hint I'll throw in a monologue on hats too.

There isn't all that much you can say about chocolate. It's great, I like it and I'll make sure that any man I'm dating knows my feelings on the subject very early on so he can buy me large boxes of the stuff.

Dogs I covered in an earlier chapter.

Every male lawyer I've ever met watches *Law & Order* as avidly as I do. This is a conversation that can go for hours especially when you ask them if they've ever been involved in a similar case. This gives them carte blanche to yammer on about themselves which, let's face it, everyone loves to do.

As for books and films there's loads of stuff to mine from them. If a guy says he liked a particular film don't just nod and say, "yep, me too". Ask him why. If he mentions a particular book, don't immediately jump in with "I read that. What a load of nonsense – it was bloody terrible." Remember you're trying to be as positive as you can because negativity is not attractive. Apart from that, if you say something derogatory about the book it's guaranteed that:

A. He wrote it.
B. His best friend wrote it.

C. It's his favourite book ever and he wishes he
   had written it.

So think before you start running it down. Forget dating;
that's just common sense. Never ever run anything or anyone
down to a person whom you don't know. Statistics show
that nine times out of ten (that's 90%) the person you are
speaking to will be the mother/sister/best friend of the one
you are bitching about. This is very bad for your health,
especially if they deck you. Being positive isn't all about
being more attractive – it's about keeping yourself out of
casualty too.

Casting Call

Whenever I do an interview with a celebrity I always ask
them who they would cast to play themselves in a movie and
why. The answers are always interesting and, more often
than not, very illuminating. Who a person would choose to
cast as themselves in a film can tell you a lot about them. It
is a good indicator if someone is deluded about himself, has
grandiose notions, a good sense of humour or, the worst
one in my book, is being falsely modest.

A tall handsome man might answer you with someone
improbable like Danny DeVito. He could be having a laugh
or maybe he's a huge fan and casting him would be a way to
meet him. Then again a 5' 6" tub of lard might want Brad
Pitt, "because we look so alike.". Then there's the chaps
who would cast themselves – watch out for those lads; their
egos are even bigger than lard–boys waistline.

Even if a guy refuses to answer you or play along, he's giving you some very valuable information about himself. Basically if you like a bit of fun and like using your imagination this might not be the best fella for you.

It ain't what you say

Non-verbal communication is just as important as what you say. Psychologists describe a process known as 'mirroring' where a couple who are really into each other will automatically and unconsciously mirror the actions of each other.

Couples who are attracted to each other not only subconsciously mimic each other's actions but they quite literally gravitate towards each other. When both of you are into each other, you will find yourself (again subconsciously) leaning in towards each other. Your body will angle itself towards his and vice versa. If you're out with a chap who's legs are facing away from you and he hasn't uncrossed his arms all evening then call for the bill.

Another sign to watch for is dilated, (widened) pupils, which generally indicate that someone is feeling pretty amenable toward you. However, watch out because alcohol and certain drugs also dilate pupils and under those circumstances it's easy to misread signals.

Oh No, Pinocchio

On the opposite end of the spectrum if someone is fidgety, constantly checking his watch and looking anywhere but at you then that's a pretty good indicator that he's not all that interested whatever his mouth might be saying.

Once upon a time anthropologists said you could tell when someone was lying to you by their giveaway body language. 'Tells' (gestures which indicated a fabrication) included tugging on the ear, rubbing the nose and placing a hand over the mouth when speaking. Current research is now contradicting all of that and saying there is no way short of a polygraph to tell if someone is lying. Even lie-detector machines aren't all that reliable when it comes down to it.

So how can you defend yourself against fairy tales? Listen very carefully and heed your gut. Your first instinct about someone is usually right. If your first reaction is 'he's dodgy' then he most probably is.

Open Season

Non-verbal communication encompasses two types of gestures – closed and open. Open gestures indicate that someone is attracted to you. Therefore you would think that closed gestures reveal the exact opposite – that someone finds you as attractive as a bad bout of flu. Wrong. Closed gestures can certainly be indicative of someone not wanting to get off with you but they could also mean that he's had a crap day and is feeling less than perky or indeed he could just be shy. Shyness is often mistaken for coldness or aloofness.

Open gestures are a definite GO sign, but be warned girls: the Internet is saturated with websites telling boys how to fake it. Why would he fake interest? Well, to get laid and laid only, unfortunately. These sites also give boys a run-down of the kind of things girls do when they're interested in order to give them the upper hand, the dirty rotten cheats.

Oooooh Sauce

Never mind, what's sauce for the gander. Take a look at these sites and apply the techniques in reverse. There are a couple of things to watch out for. One is displacement activity, when he can't hold your gaze and begins fiddling with his cuff links or adjusting his tie. Then there's mirroring. So if you deliberately rub your earlobe a few seconds later he'll rub his, or check his watch or scratch his nose – copying whatever gesture you've just made. In theory this sounds easy to fake. On one hand it is, it's quite easy to deliberately mirror someone else's actions. Alternatively it's almost impossible to restrain yourself from doing so precisely because it is subconscious.

It's good to be aware of your own body language. Nerves can result in closed gestures, in particular crossing your arms which is a protective gesture. Everyone on the planet knows about the crossed-arm gesture. Every interview guide ever published tells you to uncross your arms and the same is true of dating. No more than when you are facing an interview panel uncrossed arms say you're available and willing.

Me-itis

Don't be tempted to over-sell yourself either. While people respond well to others who are attractive and confident (fewer parking tickets apparently) there are few things as off-putting as a case of me-itis. We all know someone whose entire conversation consists of me, I said, myself, my, mine, me, me, me, meeeeeeeeeeeeeeeeeeeeeeeeeeeeeeeeeeeeeeeeeeeeeee. It's as appealing as three-day-old meat in a maggot sauce. Don't go there.

Another place to steer clear of is the overly-modest, poor-little-me room. OK let me explain. There are some people who think they're pretty great, but don't feel the need to inform everyone they meet of the fact. They're the people that have gagged their inner Carmel and locked her in a cupboard somewhere. Good for them. Then there are those who listen to every word their inner Carmel has to say and believe it. They need to get medieval on her ass and fast (see *Silencing Your Inner Carmel*). Then there's the me-itis lot. Some of them genuinely think that they're the cat's night attire and want to tell the world. Others are just trying to drown out their inner Carmel by shouting louder. They deserve your pity but not your company. Then there's the poor-little-me gang.

Poor Little Me likes to say negative things about herself but only in the hope and certain knowledge that she'll be immediately contradicted.

"Not at all, Fidelma, you are a great cook, fantastic, one of the best."

"Maura, what are you taking about? You are not fat. You look fabulous?"

"Oh, Jean, what do you mean you have no head for figures? You are a mathematical genius, Einstein himself has nothing on you."

If you have, or think you have, *Poor Little Me* tendencies this is bad, for a number of reasons.

1. This kind of shenanigans is passive/aggressive and manipulative.

2. If you fail to get the desired response it will upset you and give more ammunition to your inner Carmel.

3. Thirdly, someone might agree with you and say "Indeed, Maureen, I'm very glad you brought that up. I've been wondering for some time how to broach the subject. I'm delighted that I didn't have to be the one to tell you that you were a holy show and needed to save for plastic surgery."

I don't need to tell you what effect that would have on a girl. Suffice to say your inner Carmel would be just thrilled.

A Field Guide to the Irish Male

Pinocchio

How to Spot Him:

Unfortunately, unlike his namesake, Pinocchio's nose doesn't grow with every lie he tells. If it did, people could use it as a bridge to France. Even in the face of incontrovertible evidence, Pinocchio will refuse to admit the truth.

Habitat:

Anywhere he can spin a yarn. He is usually someplace where he is not supposed to be and will absolutely deny having been at a later date.

What he says:

Plenty and most of it is complete and utter dung. "You don't believe me!!"

What you'll never hear him say:

The truth, the whole truth and nothing but the truth.

Chapter Twenty-one

Social Intercourse

Most people Out There are just the same as you

There are measures you can take to make the most of your dating opportunity. Making conversation with a complete stranger is hard. Not every girl has the gift of small talk, but that's not necessarily a bad thing either. Having been on the receiving end of incessant witterings at social functions I'm not such a big fan of small talk myself.

Maybe you're shy. A lot of people are. One solution to shyness is to act *as if*. In other words pretend you are someone with confidence and act that way. I once had a job as a Professional Irish Person (PIP). Now the actual job itself is far too boring to get into here – suffice to say it involved going to every dog and pony show with Irish in the title in the NY area. These events covered everything from breakfasts to black-tie dinners, formal meetings to informal cocktail hours. Often I knew no one at these shindigs. Most people who know me thought this was a perfect job for me as I'm 'good at socialising' and enjoyed events like these.

I can think of few worse things than standing alone in the middle of a room where you know no one, clutching on to a glass as if your life depended on it and wondering if anyone will talk to you. Will you continue to stand there, alone, as the space around you becomes bigger and bigger until finally you are alone in the middle of the room, while everyone else is clustered around the edges pointing, laughing and calling you Norma Nomates? This is my big fear every time I attend an event on my own.

Guess how many times this has actually happened to me?

None.

The Great Pretender

Worst-case scenarios aside, the chances of being ignored or belittled are very small, so get in there with a resolve to act *as if*, pretend you are confident and happy. Look, I know just how ludicrous this sounds but trust me, it really really works. Acting happy and confident becomes a self-fulfilling prophecy. If you are so shy you can't even act *as if*, then try to fool your shy-ass brain by pretending to be someone famous. Mentally I mean. Walk into a date or a crowded room and announce you're Julia Roberts and you really will be surrounded by a lot of open space. When you arrive, plaster a smile on your face and remind yourself that everyone wants to talk to Julia, (or Nicole, Cate, or whoever your favourite celeb is).

Trust me, you can fool yourself into confidence and like most things, the more you do it the easier it becomes. OK so you're out there, beaming and dazzling and more confident than a corrupt politician on polling day. However do remember a date isn't just an opportunity to dazzle some man with how witty, attractive and generally great you are. It's also an opportunity for you to find out if this guy is worthy of your wit, charm and general loveliness. So think like a reporter and ask questions.

On A-Need-To-Know Basis

Find out what you *need* to know. Be a bit subtle though. Don't jump straight in with the big questions like "Why did your last relationship fail?" Well, fine go ahead, if you want it to be a short date. Reporters ask open-ended questions, ones which elicit a response other than 'yes' or 'no'. So instead of saying, "Do you like films?" assume he does and say, "What kind of films do you like?" No matter what the response to this question it will tell you something about him. If he says he likes big budget action films then rest assured he's a run-of-the-mill boy.

See, you could quite easily spend an evening with someone without ever having to give away the slightest bit of information about yourself at all. Although, in the interests of balance and fairness, you should give him the opportunity to ask you some stuff too.

In reality few people are boring. Most people, given half a chance, can be really interesting. Everyone has a funny story or an interesting anecdote; they may just not know it until they're asked.

Eat Your Heart Out, Miss Marple

It's important to know how a boy's previous relationships ended – or rather why. If you are looking at this chap as a serious prospect then chances are whatever finished his prior relationships is the same thing that'll end this one. OK, in an ideal world when you ask this question you'd get a truthful answer but as we all know the world ain't all that ideal. If a chap is a serial cheater and was dumped by his last three girlfriends he's unlikely to mention this. If his last relationship ended because he went to jail and his girlfriend wanted a boyfriend more actively involved in her day-to-day life it's doubtful if he'll fess up. What you may hear is 'she wanted a deeper level of commitment than I was willing to make'. If you do hear this, then for God's sake, or more importantly your own, LISTEN.

Game On

Head games are a no-no. Seriously, if you're over 14 you shouldn't be at this carry-on. People who play games are insecure and immature. Is that really the message you want to give? Games result in tests, which are never a good idea. Either he fails the test – which doesn't mean he's necessarily a bad man, just one who cannot live up to unreasonable expectations, or he gets sick of constantly having to jump through hoops and takes off. Girls aren't the only ones who play games. Think on. Isn't it tiresome when a man you're seeing keeps messing around with your head? Some people like this kind of dysfunctional carry-on. Fine, good for them. For the rest of us, it's unnecessary, it's unhealthy and it's bloody exhausting.

Go With The Flow

Conversation is supposed to be a dialogue not a monologue. It's really important to listen to what the other person is saying and not just wait for him to stop speaking. We all have our hobby-horses and pet peeves but do try to remember that not everyone is as fascinated with Paris Hilton or the reunification of Germany as you are. Also, any subject, no matter how fascinating, can become tedious after a while.

A normal conversation evolves and does not remain fixed on one subject. My friend Emma and I talk all the time. Various boyfriends have asked me, "what on earth do you find to talk about? You're always on the phone to each other." Well, basically we talk about everything. A typical conversation might begin about where one of us went for dinner the previous evening. That will lead on to a discussion of the menu. That will lead on to a debate about the merits of different Italian dishes. This will in turn lead us on to Sophia Loren, big boobs, silicone implants, L.A., surgery, anaesthesia, and on and on, until eventually one of us has to go to the bathroom and hangs up.

Listening closely to what he says will not only provide you with clues about what he's really like but will help diminish the possibility of the much feared 'awkward pause'. Say a man's employment history is more varied than a patchwork quilt and he's gone from accountancy to training for the Guards to being a roadie to gardening and now he's studying to become an aromatherapist. This man is either:

A. An actor.
B. Someone who finds it impossible to commit.

In either case you will know enough to mark his card for him.

If a man blabs on excessively about his ex, chances are he has more baggage than a conveyor belt at Dublin Airport.
NEXT.

If he bitches incessantly about his job/boss/co-workers/neighbours and tells you that everybody else is wrong and he is right then he's got as much, if not more, baggage than the previous chap.
NEXT.

If he can't talk about anything but his children/his job/computer games/the GAA/Glasgow Celtic.
NEXT.

If he doesn't shut up talking and interrupts you when you attempt to contribute to the conversation.
NEXT.

If he makes any of the following statements:
A woman's place is in the home.
A woman's place is on my face.
Bloody women drivers.
NEXT.

If he refers to women in any of the following ways –
Birds, Chicks, Cows, Tarts, Bints, Hos, Bitches.
NEXT.

If he spends the entire date roaring crying.
NEXT.

If he gets pure thick with the drink and pukes on himself/you/the taxi/ all of the above.
NEXT.

If he suggests you should lose weight or join a gym.
NEXT.

If he complains incessantly about his mother and/or has a bad relationship with her.
NEXT. (Does the name Norman Bates mean anything to you?)

I know this sounds harsh but anyone who cannot be arsed to put out their best possible self on a date is not worth the effort. Secondly, you are looking for a boyfriend not a canonisation.

Apart from listening closely to what he says for loser indicators what he says predicates what you say next. Like I said before, it's important to ask questions, to think like a reporter. However, the questions should have some relevance to the on-going conversation. Don't just come with a prepared list of standard questions to ask for the sake of asking.

How to end a date gracefully

OK, girls here's what you do. Excuse yourself from the table and go to the loo and don't return. See it's simple.

All right, I'm joking. That's exactly what not to do. How do I know this? Because in younger stupider mobile phoneless days I actually did this. I don't care how dreadful your evening is going, there is no excuse for this sort of behaviour. It's just mean. If things are so bad that you are contemplating this nasty little trick then simply be honest. Say, "Look John, I don't think this is really going very well for either of us. I'm sure you'd rather be in the pub watching the match with your friends, so let's just get the bill and call it a night."

On first sight this might sound harsh. It isn't. A well prepared girl will know exactly what sporting fixtures a man is forgoing in order to spend time with her and by offering him the alternative he will be tricked into thinking that calling it quits was his idea. Sneaky? Yes, but far more humane than leaving the poor eejit alone in a restaurant.

Another reason for avoiding the mid-date legger strategy, apart from the negative karma it will generate, is the universe being the place it is, you are bound to run into this chap sooner rather than later. You will run into him on a day when your hair is greasy. You will cross paths about two seconds after you have snagged your stockings and the stiletto heel has come loose from your shoe. You will bang into him on the street spilling your expensive coffee over your even more expensive coat but he won't notice that — he'll be too busy trying not to look at your giant cold sore and the pimple erupting on the side of your nose. He will be nothing like you remember him. He will look taller, handsomer and far better dressed. Whatever about the taller and handsomer, the better dressed will be a reality because now he's taking fashion tips from that gorgeous blonde with her arm through his. Oh yes, my little kitty-cat, a sneaky runner like this sets into motion a series of events and the inevitable outcome is exactly as I have described it. Trust me on this.

Ultimately a date will have one of two outcomes:

1. You want to see him again.
2. You never want to lay eyes on him ever again.

If it's the second of these then be polite, say, "Thanks for a lovely evening," and leave it at that. If you do want to see him again, *let him know*, tell him you had a great time and you'd love to do it again sometime. Some men can be a bit clueless about signals and need it spelled out for them.

OK, having blasted men for what they shouldn't do on dates, let's take a look at what you need to avoid.

A Field Guide to the Irish Male

The Country Boys

1. The Landed Gentry Gent

How to Spot Him:

He's wearing tweeds that have seen better years but are so old they can't actually remember them. He has a toffee-nosed English accent even though he was born and bred in Kildare (but educated in Eton). He wears wellies and drives a Range Rover that, no matter what the weather, is encrusted in mud. He's usually surrounded by three or more dogs, including but not limited to Labradors, Beagles and Bloodhounds.

Habitat:

On the back of a horse, surrounded by dogs, chasing a fox. In the Sunday supplements, photographed in the ancestral pile which he turned into a four-star hotel.

What he says:

"Tally ho." "Jolly good, what?"

What you'll never hear him say:

"One is English after all."

The Country Boys

2. Tycoon of the Townland

How to Spot Him:

He has a fine healthy complexion which a kind person will attribute to a healthy life ploughing fields and driving tractors. An uncharitable person might call it 'bar tan'. He's well-heeled and well fed. The ultimate giveaway is when he spits in the palm of his hand before shaking on a deal.

Habitat:

County fairs, cattle marts, pubs and the Party Ard-Fheis.

What he says:

"Go on, yaboyya." "Sucking Diesel." "Pulling the divil be the tail."

What you'll never hear him say:

"I'm a vegetarian."

Chapter Twenty-two

Dating Don'ts & Disasters

When Bad Dates happen to Good Girls

Dating Don'ts

Don't talk about your ex incessantly
Don't give too much airtime to any other man
Don't get rat-arsed
Don't complain about feeling tired
Don't arrange to meet in a bar where
'everybody knows your name'
Don't spend the night checking yourself out
in every reflective surface
Don't talk non-stop
Don't sit there like you've lost the power of speech
Don't bitch incessantly
Don't show-off

The Ex-Factor

Whether you are sixteen or sixty-six the man you are with at
any given moment likes to entertain the illusion that he's the
only man in the world as far as you're concerned. Nothing is

more off-putting on a first date than someone who yammers on incessantly about their ex. It screams 'unresolved business'. Speaking as a girl who has been dumped for the ex and been the ex someone else was dumped for, it's a sign you should never ignore. I don't know what's more disturbing, a person who talks longingly and wistfully about their most recent relationship, or someone who spends the night wishing all kinds of misfortune upon their previous partner. Either way it's a no-no.

The Other Man

You might well think that your Dad is the best Dad in the world, your brother is the greatest and your male next-door neighbour is just a hoot. Fine, you are most likely correct in your estimation but as with the ex-factor, your new date doesn't want to know. Too much talk about any other fella, even if he is related to you, is a big turn-off. Again, reverse the situation. If you were out with a guy who spent the better portion of the night blabbing on about some other girl, it would sicken you.

Punch Drunk

A date with a new boy is a nerve-wracking experience and nobody could blame you for wanting to take the edge off. Grand but watch how much you imbibe. None of us are at our best when we're three or more sheets to the wind. Slurred speech and bad balance ain't all that attractive and let's not even think about the crapola that most of us spout after a few bevies. Apart from making you far less attractive, sound judgement is the first victim of jarring up. Whatever decisions you make at the end of a date you want them to be your own not José Quervo's. Jack Daniels might be the guy who calls the shots but you're the one who has to live with the consequences.

Tired and Testy

The flipside of nerve-wracking is excitement. If you're out with a fella for the first time and you're feeling anything less than invigorated, something is wrong. Now it could be that you've worked three shifts in a row in a busy hospital and not seen your bed for days but even if that is the case — OFFER IT UP. An admission of tiredness so early on is like a slap in the face to the poor chap who's trying hard to impress you. You may as well just kick him in the groin and tell him that he bores you to sobs.

Cheers

You might think it makes you look popular to take a boy to your regular watering hole on your first night out. You might think that knowing the barman and all of the regulars makes you look popular. It doesn't. He may well jump to the conclusion that you're an alcoholic barfly. Apart from that, some of the other regulars may be less than discreet and give the new lad information about you that he'd be better off not knowing — like when you got off with three of the barmen last Christmas Eve and threw up all over the car park.

Vanity Insanity

When you are on a date you are supposed to pay attention to the person you're out with. Spending the entire night admiring yourself in the mirror is downright rude. Any man with an ounce of sense will pass on asking you out for a second time. If you are of a vain nature keep your eyes off yourself until you go to the jacks. If you are just insecure about having lipstick on your teeth or spinach stuck between them, then you can discreetly check up in your lippie mirror.

Blab-a-thon

Verbal incontinence is often a side effect of nerves. Been there, done that, cringed all the way home. Once you become aware that you are babbling, all too often when you've been at it for a while, don't panic. Panic will just increase your nervousness and you will go into overbabble. Stop talking. Go to the loo, take a deep breath, go for a cigarette – just stop talking. Ask your date some questions that will get him talking. Remind yourself that he is just as nervous as you are and then try to enjoy yourself.

Tongue-tied

Nerves have the opposite effect on some people and instead of responding to stress with compulsive blabbing they become paralysed and unable to talk at all. The problem with this is that your poor date is left trying to conduct a conversation all by himself. Some boys will love this but those are ones that you really don't want to go out with anyway. A normal boy will find a night of uninterrupted monologue stressful in the extreme and that will severely impact your chances of a repeat date. Even if he can deal with the stress he might take your silence as lack of interest or boredom. Either way it's not all that enticing. Remember the ice-breakers from the previous chapter? Well, those are just as applicable on dates as when you're trying to score one.

An itch to bitch

Nobody's life is perfect, we've all got problems and issues but for the love of heaven, keep a lid on it. Listening to someone slag off everyone and everything indiscriminately is about as attractive as bad body odour. Keep it positive. If you have a horrible job and hate your boss then don't talk about work. If your mother is crazy and should be in an institution just hold those thoughts for your close friends. The exception to this is when it's really really REALLY funny. Even then don't milk it.

The show mustn't go on

Well, who knew you could speak fluent French and had an intimate understanding of fine wines. Being talented and smart is great and nobody is suggesting that you play down your accomplishments but go easy. Nobody likes a show-off. Ordering in French anywhere outside of France is overkill, as is returning the wine three times.

Terrible Tales of Dating Disasters

Sometimes a date is just beyond your control. You do your best, ask questions, act positive, don't patronise the staff or criticise the wine but still . . .

A disastrous date isn't the end of the world. If you get nothing else out of it at least you'll be able to give your girlfriends a bit of a giggle with the gory details. In the meantime here a few tales of dodgy doings to be going on with.

Siobhan's worst date was when she was in her early twenties and went for dinner with a colour-blind painter. OK, just to let you know, the fact that he was colour-blind has no bearing what-so-ever on what happened between himself and Siobhan. Well, maybe it does. The fact that a man who is colour-blind decided to become a painter does tell you something. Anyway, back to the disastrous date. The colour-blind painter invited

211

Siobhan to dinner at his sister's house, way out in the wilds of the country. Despite the fact that the sister knew well in advance Siobhan was coming there wasn't enough food — not near enough. "There were three couples and four pork chops," Siobhan explained. "His sister didn't even offer to make more vegetables or anything." They weren't offered dessert either.

After dinner Siobhan went back to the painter's family home (also in the wilds of the countryside) with him. After having intimate relations for the very first time in the spare room Painter Boy snuck back to his own room. Siobhan thought that a little bit strange; he was over twenty-one after all. After a bad night, she couldn't sleep with hunger, she got up the following morning to discover that there was no food in the house for breakfast. "Nothing," she said, "no cereal, no bread, no coffee, nothing."

Siobhan had to wait ages on her bus and it was over an hour before she got home. By that time she was distracted with hunger and swore to herself she would never see Painter Boy again. "I can't say the date left a bad taste in my mouth," she said. "I would have needed to have eaten something for that to happen."

Not eating was also the cause of one of Fiona's many abortive first dates. Her hairdresser set her up with a chap whom she arranged to meet in a bar. They ordered drinks and exchanged pleasantries. They'd been in the bar about twenty minutes when out of nowhere her date says, quite conversationally, "I want to eat out your . . .,". Fiona didn't hang around for him to get to the end of the sentence. "It's not that I'm in any way opposed to that particular act," she

When Bad Dates happen to Good Girls

explained, "but generally I'd like to know someone longer than twenty minutes before discussing it."

Another date ended before it even got started. Fiona was set-up with a very rich and handsome fella. The chap gallantly offered to pick her up at her flat. When she opened the door and said her hellos he told her that she was lucky he was taking her out, 'considering you're not even a model'. Fiona was gracious enough not to bring up the fact that his dad had made his money from tampons.

Aoife once had lunch with a man who paid for the meal in loose change. She had to sit and watch patiently as he counted out a not insubstantial sum in coppers. "I just wanted the ground to open up and swallow me," she said.

Wrong attitude, I say. She should have been wishing for the ground to open up and swallow him.

Tina's big date with a doctor quickly turned sour when he made a song and dance about finding his wallet to pay for theatre tickets. "He kept patting his pockets and rummaging inside his jacket. He was taking forever so I handed him the money. Although I was fresh out of uni and stony broke I didn't actually mind paying. It was when he pocketed the change that I decided our first date would be our last."

See, bad dates happen to the nicest of girls. However, none of the girls I spoke to gave up after one bad date. The worst date I ever had happened not long after I moved to New York. I got all dolled up expecting to be taken to a fancy restaurant and instead I got dragged around the Met Museum. The shoes I had on were the type that were for show and not for schlepping. After an hour and a half, my date cheerily informed me he was late to meet some friends for dinner and left. I was abandoned in Egyptian Antiquities with my sore feet, growling tummy and an awful feeling of having screwed up somehow. Did that stop me from going out ever again? The hell it did.

Far from it, I went on to other dates, some of which actually became relationships. That's when the fun really started.

A Field Guide to the Irish Male

Goatee Beatnik

How to Spot Him:

As the name suggests he'll be sporting some effort of a goatee. GB thinks of himself as 'an artist'. He's a poet, painter or thespian. He often wears a black beret (it's post ironic, dude) and never leaves home without a notebook and a pen; you never know when the muse will strike. He has a faraway thoughtful gaze perpetually on his face.

Habitat:

Art Galleries, coffee shops with open mic nights, fringe theatres.

What he says:

He doesn't say all that much. He likes to let his "work speak for itself".

What you'll never hear him say:

"I think Brecht and Beckett are a load of bollocks."

Part Five

So Now What?

Should I stay or should I go?

Chapter Twenty-three

Next?

Ask not for whom the phone rings

The Time Traveller's Girlfriend

There are two outcomes to any date. You either want to see him again or you don't. Let's take a look at the first option for a moment. You're a modern girl; you're not going to sit around and wait for him to call you. So you went out on Saturday night, by God you'll call him at half past eight on Sunday morning, and to hell with the begrudgers.

Right then, off you go. Don't be at all surprised if he hangs up on you and you never hear from him again. New boys aside, you should never call anyone before 11:00 am at the weekend. Generally boys aren't as evolved as girls, so wait and give him a chance to call you. Some men think nothing of calling a week later. This seems like an eternity to most girls, but men and women, apart from being from different planets, also view the passage of time very differently.

If you don't hear from him by the Wednesday following your date, then make plans for the coming weekend. If he calls and finds out that you already have plans, he'll soon learn.

If he doesn't call at all you either sulk, shrug it off, or call him.

Why would I call him when he didn't call me?

Like I said earlier who knows why he didn't call you. He might have had a last-minute attack of shyness and be delighted that you made the running. Or not. The thing is, you won't find out until you try.

A few years ago I went on a date with a guy. Everything went brilliantly, there were no awkward silences and he even suggested a second date before we'd even finished our meal. There was definite chemistry and at the end of the night we gave each other a peck on the cheek and departed with a 'see you soon'. I had no doubt he would call. He didn't. So I called him and got his machine. I left a message with my number and I never heard from him again.

Who knows what happened after he left the restaurant. He could have met his ex-girlfriend and started seeing her again. He could have been hit on the head and been suffering from amnesia. It doesn't really matter. What did I lose by calling him? Nothing. At least I wasn't left with any regrets about not following up.

Why Me?

The nervous jitters you have before a date are nothing compared to the ones after.

222

Will he call?

When will he call?

Why hasn't he called yet?

What if he doesn't call?

If he doesn't call, you will shrivel up with shame and die alone. Your life will be over and the future, such as it is, is one where you will eke out your last days a spinster surrounded by thousands of yellowing newspapers, hundreds of feral cats and the stench of urine (yours, the cats, a mixture of both, who cares it still stinks).

Yes, love, that's exactly what will happen.

Get a grip will you.

Let's deal with the worst-case scenario first. You have a date with a man and everything went really well. And now it's a week later and he still hasn't called.

What is your first response? Well, if you are anything like I used to be you will assume that you are as attractive as someone with advanced leprosy, a cold sore and severe halitosis. Then you'll take to the bed with several bars of chocolate and swear off dating for ever and ever. And you'll be completely overreacting.

If you go out with someone and he doesn't call, this is a perfect opportunity to reinforce any lingering self-doubt you have. Do try to remember that the loser who didn't ring you isn't the one responsible for making you feel bad about yourself. You are. It's your own negative thinking which is making you doubt your worth as an attractive woman and a valuable member of society.

Love Lottery

If you play Lotto on a Saturday night and your numbers don't come up, is that it? Do you swear off the National Lottery and refuse to even enter a newsagent's again? Well, it's the same with giving out your number to someone you like. Sometimes we misread signals and on the other hand there are times *we don't* yet there's still no follow up phone call. Under these circumstances you simply cannot allow yourself to take the rejection personally.

Let's face it, if a guy doesn't call after a date the chances are that you weren't all that interested anyway. Seriously. Now the fact that he's unavailable is making him seem really desirable. It is a rare occurrence that a man will fail to call if the air between you zinged when you met. Rare, but it does happen. On those unusual occasions when a girl clicks with someone and they fail to follow up, the girl in question is likely to become a self-flagellating mess, blaming herself entirely for his silence.

For example, my friend Emma recently met a chap and instantly clicked with him. They chatted for hours, found themselves in agreement on just about every subject and had so much chemistry that the air between them crackled. So when he completely failed to call, Emma was very upset. "We got on so well," she said. "We had definite chemistry," she wailed. Then she went into the next phase that we girls know oh too well. Self-doubt and blame.

Just My Imagination?

Emma started to think that she had imagined the whole thing. Then she went a step further into the whole blaming-herself routine. If she was prettier, if she was funnier, if she had said 'this' if she hadn't said 'that'. And all the time these swipes at herself were punctuated with 'why?'

WHY didn't he call me?

WHY didn't he like me?

WHY am I such a complete and total loser?

WHY me?

WHY do I always get the sticky end of the lollipop?

WHY WHY WHY?

Look, unless you're a *Basic Instinct* Bunnyboiler type then you know when you click with someone. You know when there's mutual chemistry. It's there or it isn't and there's no denying it when it is. So why if there is definite, no-doubt-about-it-chemistry would he fail to call?

Here are some reasonable explanations.

After your date he was in a horrific accident on the way home and he's dead.

After your date he was in a horrific accident on the way home and he's in a coma.

After your date he was in a horrific accident on the way home and he's suffering from amnesia.

All perfectly logical explanations.

All extremely unlikely to be the truth.

Maybe his wife and/or girlfriend wouldn't let him call.

Bad Girl

I could spend the rest of this book speculating. God knows I've spent enough time doing it in the past. Hasn't every girl?

Ultimately we all come up with the same answer: we're not good enough. We're not pretty enough; we're not funny enough; we're not sexy enough. We didn't try hard enough; we tried too hard. We didn't dress up enough; we were overdressed. We weren't nice enough to his friends; we were too nice to his friends and on and on and on.

Honestly, it's exhausting and ultimately pointless. What girl has time for that sort of endless speculation? We have far better things to be getting on with, or at least we should have. Let me tell you something else: you won't find men doing this. Here's the big difference between women and men, apart from standing up or sitting down to wee.

Men Don't Blame Themselves

Earlier this year when the weather was really bad I went out very early one morning to get a cup of coffee and a bagel. It was so early that my usual coffee place wasn't even open so I went into the local 24-hour garage. Because of the ferocious weather and the ridiculously early hour I dressed thinking only of staving off hypothermia and not vanity. I looked like a 12-year-old boy in jeans, a puffy anorak, runners, all of my hair shoved under a woolly cap and a face totally devoid of makeup.

When I went to pay for my purchases the slithery little yoke behind the cash register said he wanted my number. To add insult to injury he refused to part with my bagel until he got it. Now if you met this creature you'd know that I'd rather have poked myself in the eye with a rusty screwdriver than go out with him. Honest to God, you'd wonder if his own mother had any time for him. In the interests of full disclosure I was so hungry I nearly caved, but eventually I liberated my bagel and went on my way.

What was my reaction to all of this? Did I think 'God, I must be a complete babe. Here I am at 5:30am on a snowy morning, dressed like a 12-year-old boy and men still find me desirable.'? Not at all. Instead I thought 'I must be a pretty worthless specimen of womanhood if a nerdy little creep like that thinks he has a snowball's chance in hell with me'. When I told this story to an old boyfriend he laughed. He said this is the essential difference between men and woman. If a man gets chatted up by a woman who is a bit skanky and not all that attractive, he doesn't immediately think it's a negative reflection of himself, that this is all he's worthy of. No, he instead thinks, "Boy, I am truly a Sex God."

Am I bothered?

When you have a date with a man and he doesn't call, do try to remember that in reality it probably has very little to do with you and not to use it as an excuse to join a nunnery. Rejection happens to everyone. It will not kill you. It will not bother you in the slightest unless you let it. Better it should be over after the first date than months later when you've invested time and effort into this worthless specimen who is not worth a second thought. Now on to the next one.

On the other hand, you've had one date with this bozo and

that was enough. You would be happy never to see him again. First the bad news; he's bound to call. I swear to God but every time I've gone out with a man and come home wishing I'd stayed in and cleaned the toilet he's been on the blower the next day telling me what a fabulous time he had and how wonderful he thinks I am. What the?

OK, so if you have no interest you can:

1. Simply ignore his calls, let the answering machine pick up and never call him back.

2. Change your number and purchase a new mobile.

3. Be honest.

Option three is obviously the one we should all strive for. Like a coward, I've often let my answering machine deal with these boys. We've all done that, haven't we? It's pretty much the same thing as a boy who doesn't phone. So let's try to remember in romance we girls can be just as mean and cowardly as the boys. And in future let's try to be a bit nicer to them, whether they deserve it or not.

A Field Guide to the Irish Male

Wandering Willy

How to Spot Him:

Wandering Willy isn't always conventionally attractive. More often than not he's rather ordinary-looking. It's his lack of confidence in his looks that compels him to bolster his self-esteem by making perpetual conquests. He is indiscriminate about the type of woman he'll bed; no one is too old, too ugly or too drunk for him. The only 'type' he has is one with a pudenda and a pulse. Wandering Willy is usually quite a charmer; he'll make you laugh your knickers off.

Habitat:

Anywhere he can chat up a woman, bars, clubs, health clubs, bus stops, a Wandering Willy never stops.

What he says:

"We can just hold each other."

What you'll never hear him say:

"I'd love to meet your parents."

Chapter Twenty-four

Sex & The Sensible Girl

Should I stay or should I go?

So what's the deal with intimate relations? Should you sleep with a boy on the first night or not? Well, opinion varies on that one and ultimately it's down to the individual. It also depends on what you're looking for.

Let's say you go out with a guy and you find him reasonably attractive but you don't think he's the 'one'. If you are happy enough just to get laid then what's stopping you? Just remember this cuts both ways. So if you are looking at your date as a potential BF then it's best to hold off on the getting naked until you know him a bit better. There are two reasons for this.

1. The Double Standard

Now look, I don't want to hear a load of whingeing about how I'm reinforcing a bunch of sexist stereotypes. I'm not. But I'm not going to ignore the reality of the situation. There are chaps out there who no matter how much they like a girl, will immediately classify her as easy

230

if she puts out on the first date. Sorry, babe, I know it's unfair but it's a fact.

2. Bonding

Again I can hear the clamour of a thousand feminists but the truth of the matter is women and men respond differently to the sexual act both emotionally and psychologically. After being intimate most girls will be far more bonded to a man than they were before. The reasons for this lie back when we all lived in caves and are far too complicated to get into here. Basically if you sleep with a man too soon, before you get to know him, and he's not right for you, you might end up enduring a useless relationship because of that initial bonding. Been there, done that, bought the hair shirt.

The important thing before sleeping with someone is to know your own mind. Contrary to what everyone told you when you were a teenager, you don't have to be in love to have sex. If you are simply after sex then fine. But are you? A lot of girls mix up sex with affection and love. If this is you, then be very careful because if you are rejected in the aftermath of a quick liaison it will undo whatever temporary high you got from the encounter and leave you feeling far worse in the long-term.

If your goal is just to have sex for the sake of having sex, you need to be sure of two things:

1. Your partner is aware of this and is OK. Using people, for any reason, is just not on. You don't like it when it's done to you so don't do it to others. And, it's very bad karma.

231

2. Be 100% honest with yourself – are you really OK
   with just sex. If you are in denial about your real
   motives, you will end up making yourself miserable.

If you have sex with someone in the expectation of kick-starting a relationship, be aware that it may not work that way. If some one offers me a big cream cake, I'm going to eat it. If they expect me to buy the bakery afterwards, then it's a poor look-out for them.

FBs

There is a compromise between having one-night stands and being in a committed relationship. Enter the FB.

There are two definitions for FB both essentially meaning the same thing.

1. The F is a four letter word that rhymes with 'luck'.
   The B stands for Buddy.

2. The F is for Friend, B for Benefits and there's a
   small ignored 'w' for with.

The FB relationship is a good one to cultivate if you want to take care of the physical side of things while looking for Mr. Right. Be warned though; it is difficult to find the balance in this kind of sophisticated arrangement. You need to be scrupulously honest with yourselves and each other. If there is any expectation of a more committed relationship on either side then it simply won't work.

Also with this type of arrangement both the F and the B parts are equally important. This guy really should be someone you like and respect and vice versa. That will make being honest with each other and treating each other properly all that much easier. Occasionally the FB relationship develops into something more. *Occasionally*. That's why it's important to be thoroughly honest. If you start developing deeper feelings for your FB, you need to tell him. Either he will be delighted or horrified. You cannot just carry on as you are. That is being really unfair to yourself and to him. He doesn't know the rules have changed and therefore cannot provide you with what you really want and in the end everyone will suffer for it.

> *Ursula has been going out with a chap called Winston for the past six years. During those six years her best friend Janie got married and had a child. Ursula was at the wedding and the christening. Winston wasn't. In fact, Janie has never met Winston. None of Ursula's friends have met him. Janie actually thought Ursula was making him up until he answered the phone to her one morning.*

> *Ursula and Winston never go to the cinema together. They don't go to parties or for dinner. They never go out at all. Every Friday night around 11:00 pm Winston arrives at Ursula's apartment and gives her a good seeing to. Sometimes he spends the night, sometimes he leaves. Despite all of this Ursula refers to Winston as her BF.*

Girls, this is not a relationship. Winston is not Ursula's boyfriend, he's not even her FB. What this is is the world's longest *Booty Call*. Ursula and Winston should be in the record books. The thing is, though, Ursula has herself convinced that this man, who she shares nothing with except on occasion bodily fluids, who has no commitment towards her, whose friends she's never met and whom her friends wouldn't know if he stood under a sign saying 'Winston', is her boyfriend. Now that's denial.

Desirable Devices

If you've been single for a while and can't find a suitable FB, you don't necessarily need to hop into bed with the first fella that happens by. A girl can (and should) take matters into her own hands. If your own hands aren't doing it for you, there are all manner and make of devices around.

Get your hands on one and use it. It will, to quote my married lady friend Vanessa, "take the bitter look off your face," and more importantly if you are taking care of your physical needs yourself you are more likely to make a better choice about the man you want to date long-term.

There is nothing dirty, slutty, shameful or desperate about owning and using a vibrator. It just makes sense. A word of warning though: devices are not for sharing. I don't mean in the bedroom sense – many couples use sex toys in bed. What I mean is the actual physical sense. For hygiene purposes your device should not be used by any one else.

Holy Trinity

There's a school of thought that subscribes to having three boys on the go at the same time.

Boy Number One

The FB, his sole purpose is to be available for booty calls and to take care of your sexual needs.

Boy Number Two

The Listener, a tame *Feathery Stroker* who will listen to all of your worries and angst.

Boy Number Three

The Date, the possible candidate for a relationship. With your physical and emotional needs already taken care of you can concentrate on getting to know the potential BF and see if he really is Mr. Right.

So you think you may have decided on Mr. Right. When is the right time to start getting naked? Read on.

A Field Guide to the Irish Male

Betty Embrace

How to Spot Them

Habitat

What he Says

What you'll never hear him say

A Field Guide to the Irish Male

Betty Bothways

How to Spot Him:

It's not all that easy to spot a Betty. Unless you see him snogging another guy and then five minutes later feeling up a lassie you're likely to remain ignorant about his free-for-all approach to intimate relations. The first you'll know about it is when you're actively having intimate relations with him and he casually mentions his bothwaysness in passing.

Habitat:

Anywhere people congregate with the aim of getting laid. Nightclubs, discos, gay bars, sex clubs, the gym, the supermarket, anywhere there are people who are breathing.

What he says:

Very little, he's too busy shagging everything that doesn't move quick enough, to have time to talk.

What you'll never hear him say:

"No." He's up for anything.

Chapter Twenty-five

Right On Time

So when is the right time for the first time?

Every time you have intimate relations with a new fella it's almost like losing your virginity all over again. In more ways than one. There are many of us who can't remember our first time because we were rat-arsed drunk at the time. At the risk of sounding like someone's mother – this is insanity. Getting so drunk you cannot remember exactly what you did and with whom is not only stupid, it's dangerous and it's very sad.

The first time with a guy or the very first time ever are scarifying in the extreme. It's more than understandable that a girl might want to calm her nerves with a drink or two. Just remember there's a huge difference between calming the jitters and being comatose.

Getting so bladdered that you can't remember doing it can lead to complications not least of which is whether you used contraception. Apart from the obvious health and safety issues, getting hideously drunk means that you won't be able to remember whether or not he was any good at it.

Scary Moves

Instead of trying to blot out everything that's happening, you should be savouring it. You will never be able to have sex with this person *for the first time* ever again. Believe it or not, he's scared too. Boys worry about all of the same things that girls do.

They worry that we're going to judge their bodies and their technique.

They worry about not being able to last the distance.

They worry about rogue farts escaping while they're in the middle of things.

And then there's willies. Boys have a list of worries the size of an average blockbuster novel associated with just their willies alone. In many ways, girls have it easy.

That doesn't stop you worrying. Many girls fear getting naked and being judged inadequate. Listen, it's a very odd and rare man indeed that does a critique of a naked woman's body. He's usually so thrilled to be in the same room as a nude woman that pretty much all that's going on in his brain at that moment is 'Whoo-hoo!'.

When you are having sex with a guy he is very focused on the fact that he's having sex. What small part of his brain isn't inactivated by pleasure is full to the brim with willy worries and he doesn't have space to worry about the shape of your tummy.

By the way, in the unlikely event of the man you are getting naked with having the audacity to criticise your physique then he is nothing more than a standard-issue asshole and should be dumped as soon as is humanly possible.

Another Well-Kept Secret

First-time sex is often atrocious. This is a well-kept secret. Nobody wants to admit to this in case it makes them look bad, or inadequate, or inexperienced. Don't worry if the sex is terrible. Life is not a romance novel where bodies merge together in white-hot passion and both parties come together with gasps and rasps and all other manner of clichés.

The very first time my ex, Actor Boy, and I had intimate relations it was abysmal. Truly awful. Now there were extenuating circumstances. I had just gone through two major upheavals, one in my personal life and one in my professional life. I was working fifteen-hour days and under constant pressure. I wasn't sleeping and was barely eating. I really shouldn't have been attempting to negotiate my way around a new relationship in the middle of all of that but when you meet someone and sparks fly it's kinda hard to say, "Look I'm a bit overwhelmed at the minute. Do you think you could come back when things have calmed down a bit?"

We had been dating for about three weeks when we decided to do it. There was no shortage of chemistry but it was a case of the spirit being willing but the flesh being too stressed and tense to respond. Half-way through Actor Boy ceased all activity and said, "You really don't seem to be enjoying this very much."

Yes, it was that bad. Because we had been seeing each other for a while it wasn't a total disaster. We stopped attempting to do what was clearly a bad idea, watched telly for a while and went to sleep. However, in the middle of the night...

Our subsequent sex life was pretty hot. The thing about the terrible start wasn't how awkward the initial encounter was, it was the way it was handled. Actor Boy knew I fancied him rotten and he didn't take it personally. He knew I was completely over-stressed at work and the thing I needed more than anything else was a bit of understanding and a good night's sleep. Well, at least I got the understanding.

Sex is magical but not magic

In the course of writing my column, I've often been asked what's right and what's wrong, as in what's OK to do in bed and what isn't. This is easier to answer than you might think. Two words – 'consenting' and 'adult'. Oh, and after some of the letters I've received I feel compelled to add a third – 'human'. Don't ask. Please please don't ask.

If it feels good, then it's right and if it doesn't feel good, then it isn't. Honestly, it's that simple. Basically, as long as two people are old enough to consent to sex then anything they do together is OK.

If you do something you don't feel comfortable with, then that's wrong. That is my definition of perverse. Coercion of

241

ANNE MARIE SCANLON

any kind is wrong. *There are no circumstances when using force is acceptable.*

Compromising Positions

Being uncomfortable with certain positions or acts is perfectly normal. Nobody likes everything. If you don't want to try a particular act or position that's fine and nobody should tell you otherwise. However, maybe you should take time to analyse why you don't want to attempt it. It could be that you simply don't like it, find it uncomfortable or distasteful – fine. If, however, you are nervous because of inexperience or worried about doing it wrong, then talk to your partner.

Seriously, isn't it better to tell someone why you're reticent about doing something than just doing an Ian Paisley by issuing a bald "NO" and leaving it at that?

242

A Field Guide to the Irish Male

Jon Bon Rock God

How to Spot Him:

He has gorgeous hair, long and flowing, with amazing natural highlights that girls admire and envy. He is usually clad head to foot in denim but on special occasions he'll break out the leather trousers, which are far too tight around the crotch.

Habitat:

Smoky gigs, hard rock festivals, biker bars and the hair product aisle in the chemists. Once a month Jon can be found in a hair salon miles away from his home (where nobody will recognise him), getting those natural lights reapplied.

What he says:

"There haven't been any decent records released since 1975."

What you'll never hear him say:

"Short back and sides, please." "I think Ronan Keating is a genius."

Chapter Twenty-six

Bediquette

The ins and outs of proper bedtime behaviour

Oh, all right then, I'll make it a little bit easier for you. Here's some does and don'ts for behaviour in the scratcher, otherwise known as *Bediquette*.

When I talk about behaviour in bed I'm not referring to the act of intimate relations. There are so many sex manuals around and so much public discussion about the act that there is no excuse these days for not being 'good in bed'. Therefore I am not going to get into a detailed discussion of sexual technique and 'moves'.

Thrilling The Ears

Sex is about enjoying all five senses – sound, sight, taste, smell and touch. Now once you're naked and in bed with someone, you've basically got all of them covered except for sound. Sound doesn't necessarily mean *Talkin' Dirty*. Non-verbal sounds can be just as powerful as the spoken word, especially in the context of sex. Of course, some people like to use words in bed and that's grand. Not all bed-talk is dirty talk. There's a big difference between gasping "I love you" and growling "I love it when you stick your big cock into me," or something similar. Depending on who you are and who you're with, both approaches can be equally effective. Dirty talk can also encompass complicated fantasies with involved scenarios. Personally I find a running commentary distracting and quite boring but again each to their own.

Auditory cues are very important so don't hold back. If you feel like making a noise or saying something then go for it. If you don't know what to say then state the bleedin' obvious. If he has a lovely lad, tell him. If he has a perfect bum, say so. If he does something which feels good, let him know. This has the double effect of enhancing the current act and all future encounters because he will know what you like.

Basically going to bed with someone is about enjoying yourself and ensuring they enjoy themselves. You cannot do this if you're self-consciously 'performing'. Just relax and let it happen, but try if possible to bear in mind the following.

DON'T ever discuss your number (as in the number of men you've been with) with a boy. The only time you should discuss your sexual history with a man is if you took away mementoes from previous lovers i.e. children or diseases. These are things a man should be told about; anything else is none of his business. Trust me, no matter what the answer it will be the wrong one.

DON'T ask a man his number. Why do you want to know? What difference will it make? None that's what. Also if you ask him and then he turns around and asks you how many boys you've known intimately you can hardly refuse to answer him. Just leave the numbers for your Lotto ticket and move on.

DON'T compare the man in your bed with any other men who may have been there before him. (This applies to sofas, kitchen worktops, boardroom tables, the sea, the beach and anywhere else intimate relations might have occurred.) If he asks, refuse to answer. This is an explosion waiting to happen and not the type of bedroom explosion so beloved of romance novelists. Steer clear of all comparisons, making them or asking yourself.

DON'T criticise the size/shape of his lad. This is just cruel. A lad isn't like a jumper, he didn't choose that particular model himself and there is little can be done to change it, so be nice. If his lad isn't to your liking keep schtum about it. You have the option of trading one lad for another; he doesn't.

DON'T ask him what he's thinking before, during or after sex. In fact don't ever ask him this. You won't want to hear the answer. He's probably quite happily musing on one of the following.

1. Beer or other types of alcoholic beverages.
2. What he's going to eat next.
3. Football.
4. His willy.
5. Your boobs.

The chances that he's lying there thinking how wonderful you are, how lucky he is and how much he loves you are far more slender than your average Hollywood starlet.

A postcoital mind is a remarkably clear one, not in the sense of concise thinking but in the sense of empty. If you've actually done the sexual act properly you're generally in that blissed-out feel-good state that is beyond focusing and all kinds of mad random thoughts come and go, none of which actually mean anything. In that condition you are quite likely to think about anything at all from, 'aren't flowers lovely,' (seriously) to 'whoops, forgot to buy milk on the way home'. Boys are no different in this respect and if in a fit of madness they answered the 'what are you thinking about?' question honestly the chances of finding themselves outside your house with their clothes in a heap at their feet within thirty seconds are ridiculously high.

The last reason for keeping the 'thinking' question out of the bed is that it's bloody annoying. Boys as a rule don't tend to ask girls this question as soon as their post-ride breathing has returned to normal. Of course, lucky girl that I am, I managed to go out with one of the small percentage who do. I couldn't just reply, "nothing," which was usually the case because he'd badger me until he got an answer thus taking all the good out of the whole post-ride experience. Eventually I wised up, and as soon as he asked I'd say, "Oh, I'm thinking about you and how much I love you." That apparently was the right answer.

If you are in a relationship read that last bit aloud to the boy in your bed. That way if you slip up and inadvertently ask him what he's thinking he'll know the correct response.

The Morning After

How a girl behaves with a chap the morning after they've

spent the night together depends on whether the sleepover took part in his gaff or yours. In either case under no circumstances do you wrap your arms and legs around him octopus style first thing in the morning and say, "Oh I wish we could stay like this all day."

Why? Well, this is both clingy and suffocating in every sense of the words.

Get out of bed.

Yes, I know it's tempting to linger in a lovely warm bed with a lovely warm body, but now is not the time. Get up and get moving. You are a busy girl, places to go, people to see. You don't have time to be malingering in some lad's bed, or to have him camping out in yours.

Offer the chap breakfast.

I'm not suggesting for a second that you don an apron and whip up a full Irish or a batch of pancakes. A cup of tea and a slice of toast will suffice. How he responds to this offer will speak volumes about his future intentions towards you. If he stays for breakfast, chances are you're going to hear from him again. If he refuses your offer, it doesn't necessarily mean that you won't hear from him. He might actually have work commitments or a dog waiting patiently to be let out for a wee. You'll know from his reaction whether he's genuinely sorry or if he just can't wait to get the hell out of your house.

If he stays for breakfast, do not let him hang around afterwards. There will be plenty of time for that later if you continue to see each other. I've heard one too many stories from both girls and boys about spending the night and the whole of the next day with someone, only never to hear

The Morning After

from them again. It's bad enough to be blown out after you've slept with someone but it's worse when you've actually spent quality time together.

By the same token if you stay over in his place get up and get out as soon as you can. Feel free to stop for a cup of coffee en route. If he doesn't offer you coffee, or claims he has no tea or coffee in the house make plans for the following weekend because you will not be seeing lover boy again. Under no circumstances should you hang around asking him what plans he has for the day. Men hate this. He probably doesn't have any plans for the day but he can't really lounge around the house watching the *EastEnders* omnibus and scratching his groin if you are there, can he?

Relish being able to run off and do your own thing because before you know it, you'll be thrown down on the couch beside him viewing the groin scratching. Welcome to the wonderful world of relationships.

A Field Guide to the Irish Male

The Cry Baby

How to Spot Him:

Cry Baby is a Feathery Stroker who's completely lost the run of himself. He's so in touch with his feelings that they're thinking of taking out a restraining order against him. He will cry over just about anything; dog food adverts get him teary-eyed while those for cars send him into complete hysterics — "petrol fumes are destroying the environment".

Habitat:

Therapists' couches and huge bulk-buy outlets stocking up on industrial quantities of tissues.

What he says:

"Sorry, mumble mumble, sorry." It's hard to know what he says as he usually sobbing at the same time.

What you'll never hear him say:

"What a laugh!"

Chapter Twenty-seven

Going All The Way

Relationship Territory can be a scary place for the unarmed girl

Honeymoon Swoon

So you're going with him. Isn't it great? Everything is lovely, you couldn't be happier. Enjoy it. It's called the Honeymoon Period. At the beginning of a relationship you just can't get enough of each other. You have to schedule 'nights off' from each other, only to end up spending three hours on the phone and eventually either you or he will hop in a taxi and race across town in the small hours of the morning because you just can't bear being apart. It's great, isn't it? You're not only mad about him; you love everyone else too. Those few times that you're not with your beloved or talking to him you're talking about him. One of the worst things about the honeymoon period is that you get very little sleep, but it's not *the* worst thing. The worst thing about this time is that it ultimately has to end. Feck.

Be careful as well about over-bore. Your friends fully expect you to become a bit of a one-subject bore when you meet a new fella. However, realise that even your best friends have their limits. Once the honeymoon period is over your friends expect you to return to normal and not feel the urge to mention the BF's name in every sentence.

"Jim says."

"Niall thinks."

"Tony wants."

Enough! Boy Bores and Overbores don't get asked to many parties — remember that.

Apart from being blissed out, loved up and just so thrilled with each other, the other good thing about the honeymoon period is that it's a great way of screening out lousers. If a boy can't be on his very best behaviour during the first three months, then watch out. This is the time when those warning signs you missed on the first couple of dates will appear. He might have been eager to please and always on-time for the first month but how is he in the second? He might have been Mr. Generosity on the first few dates but is his wallet gathering dust a mere month or two after you met? Basically, if a boy can't be on his best behaviour with you and keep trying to impress you for three short months, it doesn't bode well for how he'll be in the future.

Tell-tale Traits

When early warning signs appear at the start of your relationship, they should not be ignored. Everyone is on their bestest behaviour when they meet someone new. Cracks appearing in the surface in the first few months will become deep crevices the longer you are together.

Some of these early warning signs are far more important than others and should *never* be ignored. If a man you're dating is less than generous with the cash when you are starting out as a couple – the time when he's supposed to be trying to impress you – then don't think your undying love is going to turn him into a philanthropist.

Another early warning sign that should send you running for the hills is a boy who's 'a bit controlling'. Generally they become a lot more controlling as time goes by. Inappropriate displays of jealousy fall into the same category. Now, in all fairness, who hasn't entertained a fantasy or two about two fellas duelling at dawn to win our affection? Again, fantasy and reality need to be considered separately.

Knowing a man finds you the 'fairest of them all' is extremely flattering. However, if he thinks every guy around is giving you the glad eye then it becomes a little less flattering and a little bit more *frightening*. This can quickly evolve to the point where you are accused of giving the come-on to all and sundry from the barman to the octogenarian at the bus stop. If you are still in this relationship at this point, then you really need to think about making a change. Jealousy and the need to control are evil and destructive. Not all controlling men will become violent but even so, you are a big girl. You shouldn't be forced to take orders from anyone. If you don't believe me, visit an abused women's shelter and you'll see just how destructive the Green-Eyed Monster can be.

If a man is jealous or controlling, don't think that all he needs is the love of a good woman to change him. He won't change. You will. And not for the better.

It's not just with potential relationships where girls can ignore their instincts to their detriment. Despite the advances of feminism over the past thirty years girls are still brought up to a certain extent to be 'nice'. Sugar and spice and all that. Girls are still reared to put the needs of others before their own (like a good Mammy). Part of being 'nice' is being discouraged from arguing, fighting or displaying anger. Now that's all fine if you are someone's Mammy. Then you will need every ounce of patience you have in order not to thump the *little darlings* on an hourly basis.

Don't talk yourself out of being reasonably afraid. Every girl has had a bad experience with the opposite sex, whether they've been followed home by crazy smelly nut-jobs or gone out with them. It's the very lucky girl that's only had one bad experience.

So what do you do when you have had a bad experience? LEARN FROM IT.

Name Game

Assuming your new chap isn't displaying any signs of dodginess, the next hurdle is when do you start calling him your boyfriend and vice versa? That's a tricky one. It's like leaving a toothbrush in each other's places – with each individual it differs. I was going out with a guy once for a month, (I even had a toothbrush to call my own in his bathroom), when he introduced me to a casual acquaintance as his 'friend.' Then he looked at me and waited for a reaction. He got one. As soon as the casual acquaintance was out of earshot I said, "So, tell me, do you sleep with all of your friends?"

With Actor Boy the girlfriend issue arose when we were watching a Monty Python promo on television. The tag line was "If your girlfriend didn't laugh at this, dump her."

"You didn't laugh," Actor Boy said.

"So I'm your girlfriend then?"

God, the romance of it all.

I don't know what it is about the words 'girlfriend' and 'boyfriend' but they're sticky. Unlike a marriage proposal it's a rare man that will ask you to become his girlfriend. The last time that happened to me I was six.

Even when you do things NY style by dating, talking and agreeing to be exclusive there's still a bit of hesitation and awkwardness about the use of the 'B' or 'G' words. I wish I could offer some useful advice at this point but I can't. Usually the 'moment' comes when you run into someone and before you get a chance to make the introductions they say, "So, is this your boyfriend/girlfriend?" Then there's an excruciating moment when you look at each other and go 'ummm'. Finally one of you will crack, say yes, there'll be a big sigh of relief all round and that will be that. Phew.

Phew, my eye. The work is just starting. For every upside there is to having a Significant Other – having someone to meet you at the airport, having someone to carry your bags from the airport, (I travel a lot so I'm a bit fixated on airports), someone to make hot drinks when you're sick yadda yadda yadda, there are as many downsides.

Your BF will probably have interests, hobbies and friends that you could live happily without. Likewise he may well think your hilarious friend from the office is the biggest pain in the arse he's ever met and about as funny as an impacted wisdom tooth. This is where you need the bedrock of shared interests and goals I spoke about earlier. You might get on famously with each other and maintain your individual social circles and interests separately. This is pretty much the ideal. You don't want to become one of those boring women whose entire focus in life is her fella. Make sure you keep your pre-relationship identity intact. Don't be one of those girls who dumps all of her female friends as soon as someone with a willy shows up. Apart from all the obvious reasons why this is a bad idea, there's the possibility that in a few weeks, months or years the relationship will end and then where will you be?

Although it's quite possible to keep whole areas of your life separate from your relationships there are some parts which sooner or later will have to be dealt with.

The Other Women

If you go out with a boy for long enough, eventually you're going to have to meet his family. If at all possible try to have the initial meeting on neutral ground, rather than the family home. There are loads of reasons why – most of them to do with territory, power positioning and other things that you can read all about in psychology and anthropology books.

OK, here's the practical reason – on neutral territory you can choose what you want to eat. Remember the list of foods that are banned on a first date? Well, that's the same list that his mother uses when she's cooking for the new girlfriend.

I don't know whether the Mammies do this purposefully or

ANNE MARIE SCANLON

not, but go to her house and you will get a plate of something that is impossible to eat without making a holy show of yourself and destroying her good tablecloth into the bargain. "Oh, don't worry about it," she'll say. "It's old. My grandmother got it as a wedding present."

If you have to have the introductory meal in his family home then remember this one piece of advice.

DO NOT UNDER ANY CIRCUMSTANCES SAY
YOU ARE STARVING.

Let me explain why. I went to a chap's house once and announced just prior to dinner that I was absolutely ravenous. Then the food arrived. It looked OK, it smelled OK and it was completely inedible. I tried the old anorexic's trick of cutting it up and moving it around my plate but there is no fooling an eagle-eyed Mammy.

"I thought you said you were hungry?" she said in an accusatory tone. She was a very nice woman and if I hadn't made it so obvious that I found her cooking repulsive we probably would have gotten on really well. However, that was not the case and, let me just add, piss off the mother and you piss off the son.

Separation Agreement

If you are unfortunate enough to have to go out of town to meet the family, the chances are you will be staying in the house. God help you is all I can say. This is a minefield.

First of all there are the sleeping arrangements. Abide by

them. A night in a bed, or pullout sofa, alone won't kill you. Remember it's their house and they are perfectly entitled to make whatever rules they please. I know people who make their guests remove their shoes at the front door. Personally I think this is a bit stupid but it's their house – they're allowed. In my house I wouldn't care who slept with who but fail to use a drink coaster and you're in deep trouble. Well, in fairness, who wants big water rings all over their furniture?

If you and your beloved are placed in separate rooms, think of it as something which is going to enhance your sex life no end.

1. The enforced abstinence will make sparks fly when you do actually get together.

2. You can use this as an opportunity to get together as the opportunity arises, which is always very exciting.

Alfresco Fiasco

OK, a quick word about opportunity arising. If you decide to have sex outdoors you run the risk of getting caught. This is all part of the thrill, I know. Think on. If you are discovered by a Garda you could find yourself facing charges. To ensure that you don't make a bad situation worse be polite, agreeable and don't smart-mouth them. In fact, no matter what the circumstances giving lip to cops is not a good idea.

The Mammy is just one of the other women you'll have to deal with when you start going with a boy. If he has sisters the chances are that they will be mini-Mammies and you'll need to work just as hard impressing them. Then there's the other woman or women. The ex-girlfriends.

The EX Files

There are three things a man will inevitable say about his ex.

1. She was so beautiful she could have been a model.

2. She was a complete psycho.

3. She was so beautiful she could have been a model but she was also a complete psycho.

These statements are not to be taken literally. Remember for every man who says any of the above to you, some other man is saying exactly the same things *about* you to someone else.

Emma once went out with a fella who had been with his previous girlfriend for six years. He was still friends with the ex, which was threatening enough but whenever he spoke about her he brought up the fact that she was so beautiful she could have been a model. This ate away at Emma who is herself a gorgeous woman. She had visions of this girl in her head that made the average supermodel look like a pig wearing lipstick by comparison. Then after she'd been going out with this guy for almost a year she came across a picture of the ex. Was she stunningly beautiful? Was she more competition than a mere mortal could handle? Was she hell. "She had a face like a plate," Emma, who is generally not given to unkindness, said. "She wasn't just not beautiful; she was pretty hideous."

Emma felt, quite rightly, that she had been jipped. The man in question was playing a very nasty game indeed. He was letting her know that she could never live up to the paragon of loveliness that he had previously gone out with. In other words Emma was lucky to have him. The same is true when a man says his ex is a psycho; it's a way of telling you not to rock the boat or you too will be labelled as a mad bitch from hell.

The GEM

Not the diamond, the *Green-Eyed Monster*. Being jealous of the ex is perfectly normal. Being suspicious of the ex if she and your BF are still friends is also perfectly normal, and also quite sensible. It's all too easy to resume relations with an old sexual partner and you know well that you've done it yourself. Apart from that there is nothing that makes a man seem more desirable than another woman fancying him.

Do not fall into the trap of being bitchy and mean to and about the ex.

A. You will alienate her and give her more reason to rekindle their romance (if it can be rekindled).

B. You will annoy him.

You may well have a perfectly platonic relationship with your ex and you wouldn't like it if your current BF started slagging him off and taking every opportunity he could to score points against him.

If you are lucky enough to be put into contact with your BF's ex, don't blow it. Yes, *lucky*. Make it your business to befriend this woman, seek her company and be nice to her. She is a source and short-cut to all sorts of information about your BF that it would either take you years to uncover or indeed never find out at all. In all likelihood she will tell you the real reason why their relationship didn't last.

Now sometimes it isn't all that easy to befriend the ex. Sometimes the ex doesn't quite get that she is actually the ex.

My friend Niamh's early relationship with her now husband was almost a threesome. "No matter where we went," she said, "his ex Bernie would turn up." Not only would Bernie show up but she would monopolise Fergus, Niamh's boyfriend. "Inevitably she'd start roaring crying," Niamh recalled. "Then all her friends would start comforting her and Fergus is just too nice for his own good so he'd be trying to make her feel better too. Meanwhile I'd be left sitting there completely ignored."

Bernie didn't stop with accidental-on-purpose meetings. She would call Fergus at 1 or 2 am 'just to talk'. Whenever Niamh went out of town Bernie would arrange to meet Fergus. Things got worse when Bernie told Fergus that Niamh had been bad-mouthing her and telling anyone who would listen about her private business. "That was it," Niamh said. "I was sick of being nice. Whenever she arranged to meet Fergus I made damn sure I showed up too. Eventually she got the message."

OK, so sometimes you will have a fight on your hands. Niamh did exactly the right thing. Bernie was pretty good at playing the victim and eliciting sympathy. She kept playing on Fergus's good nature and his guilt about breaking up with her to keep in contact with him. If Niamh had bitched about her it would have backfired because Fergus would have felt even more sympathy for Bernie. In the end Bernie had to lie about Niamh's alleged bitching and even then Niamh didn't react. She just quietly asserted herself in her role as the girlfriend.

If you do find yourself in a position similar to Niamh's then know your adversary. Figure out what game she's playing and then refuse to take part. Nothing ruins a game more quickly than someone who says, "I won't play."

Fighting Fit

Eventually the honeymoon period has to end. At some point you're going to have a fight with your beloved. This is inevitable and does not necessarily mean that it's over. Fights are awful but making up is usually great fun. Once you're full swing into a relationship, make-up sex is usually pretty great. Why wouldn't it be? Blood pumping, adrenaline rushing, it's a reminder of what the sex was like when you first met.

The downside of make-up sex is that you can get hooked and start using fights as a kind of foreplay. This isn't a great way to maintain a healthy relationship.

No matter how often or little you fight with your BF, do try to keep the battles private. Public brawling is never a good idea unless you are a drunken rock star with serious drug issues, then it's obligatory. Apart from the obvious reasons for keeping your disagreements behind closed doors you don't want to go public because you are severely limiting your chances of hooking up again if this relationship fails. There may well be a fella who fancies you but seeing you roaring swear words at another chap in the street will soon put paid to that.

Your Place Or Mine?

The longer you're going out with someone the more time you spend in each other's gaffs. One of the first signs that you're both in this thing for the long haul is when your respective toothbrushes take up residence in each other's bathroom. After a while the toothbrush is no longer your sole ambassador in his gaff – a couple of pairs of knickers are busy carving out a space of their own in the bedroom.

If a man hasn't told you that he loves you but offers you your very own drawer and an entire shelf in the bathroom, then fear not. He's crazy about you. For a man to take the time and effort to clear space for your stuff means he's beyond smitten.

However, while you are both still living apart remember that apart from that one shelf and drawer his flat is *his* space and should always be respected as such. If he's a messy pig then don't feel like you have to rush in with a mop and pail. Apart from everything else you are not his Mammy. You are his girlfriend and it is not your job to do any of the following:

His washing-up.
His laundry.
His ironing.
His cleaning.
His hoovering.

If he's living in muck there are ways of dealing with it, without having to get your hands dirty. A few years ago I was going out with a fella who was disgustingly messy. Eventually I couldn't ignore it any longer. I gave him an ultimatum – he could clean up or he could sleep alone.

If you don't fancy being this brutal, then you can always suggest to the BF that he should hire a cleaner to come in and do what he is unwilling or unable to do.

Moving On and In

After a while living apart seems a bit stupid, especially if you have to lug a hairdryer back and forth from his gaff a couple of times a week. Apart from the romantic reasons there are plenty of practical ones too. Why pay two rents, two sets of gas bills, two phone bills when two people can live together as cheaply as one? Right? OK, logically this makes sense but practically if the main reason you're going to set up home with your fella is financial then think again.

Moving in together irrevocably changes a relationship. Living together is not easy. If you're feeling a bit narky or PMSy when you're going with someone, you can always postpone seeing him until you feel better. When you wake up beside him every day you don't have that option. If you are thinking of moving in with your man just think for a minute – 'do I want to spend every day with this man?' If the answer is an unequivocal YES, then go for it. If you have any doubts at all then you really need to think things over.

Then there's the little things that taken cumulatively can kill love stone-dead – who drank the last of the milk and put the carton back in the fridge? Who left the loo seat up AGAIN? Who forgot to pay the phone bill on time? Sometimes a trouble shared becomes a trouble doubled. Therefore it's a good idea to go on holiday with someone if you're thinking about moving in with him. Travel, despite the hype, is quite stressful. I'm horribly impatient and can't abide delays of any sort. Judging from the carry-on I've witnessed at airports and on planes I'm not the only one. If you can survive travelling together, you have a better chance of making a go of living together.

Once you've taken the plunge and moved in with someone, remember, that's it – you can never go back to the way things were. Have you ever heard of a couple who moved in, decided it wasn't for them and returned to living separately and just dating? If you move in together and it doesn't work out, that's it. Game over. End of.

A Field Guide to the Irish Male

Mammy's Boy

How to Spot Him:

He could easily be mistaken for a Holy Joe (often because he is one). The main difference between him and the standard issue Holy Joe is that he is accompanied everywhere by his elderly mother. Like Holy Joe he's obsessively neat and tidy. His clothes are always spick and span because Mammy buys them, washes them, irons them and, when needs be, mends them. If you have any doubts, keep watching. Eventually Mammy will spit on a tissue and wipe an imaginary mark from his face.

Habitat:

Church with the Mammy, Bingo with the Mammy, and Tea Rooms.

What he says:

"Well, Mammy says . . .,"

What you'll never hear him say:

"Shut up, Mum."

Chapter Twenty-eight

Breaking Up Is Hard To Do

Breaking up or breaking down?

No matter how well relationships begin, many of them are destined to break up. A lot of romances end because the people involved want different things. This is why it's good to know early on what you want, what you don't want and what you're willing to compromise on.

Relationships where couples are still happy with each other but want different things are hard to end, which is why you don't want to start them in the first place. There are few things in life as hard as walking away from someone whom you love but cannot be with because your needs are different. Many of us simply cannot do it but in the end it still doesn't work. If you want to have a child and the man you are with is vehemently opposed to it, you will end up resenting him. It's better to just walk away.

If your career is your priority, there is little point in hooking up with a man whose job will demand frequent moves. If you put your relationship first, ultimately you will blame him for not progressing in your own career.

Different priorities aren't the only reasons that relationships end. Let's not forget the old favourite – the third party.

Old Dogs with New Tricks

When you've been going with someone for a while it's inevitable that intimate relations will conform to some sort of basic pattern. You will eventually get to know all his moves and little tricks, as he will know yours. That's why, if he suddenly performs a move that you haven't encountered before, I suggest you start paying more attention to what he's doing outside the bedroom.

Two women I know both found out that their respective boys were cheating after they used a new move in bed. Sex is like everything else in life; we pick up new ideas and interests from the people we meet. If a boy suddenly does something radically different in the scratcher after you've been with him a long time, the chances are he didn't get the idea from reading a gentlemen's magazine or watching a porno. Incidentally, these are the two most popular excuses used by men when they've been rumbled.

Susan never got the chance to find out if her BF had picked up any new moves. While Susan was sick in bed Owen called and left her a voicemail. Unfortunately for him he failed to disconnect his mobile and Susan had a tape of him regaling the lads, in excruciating detail, about how he had bedded another woman the night before while Susan had been tucked up in her sick bed.

269

Sometimes it's nobody's fault; a couple just drifts apart.

Breaking up is never easy whether you are the dumper or the dumpee. If you are doing the dumping, be nice about it. Don't play games or run away from the confrontation.

Now we all know that the following ways of breaking up are completely *unacceptable*.

Answering machine

Bad, very very bad. This is for complete cowards and lame brains. If you leave a message breaking up with someone, they have every right to bad-mouth you all over town as a consequence.

Fax

Even worse than the answering machine. Most of us don't have faxes at home so the most likely place you will receive a fax is at work. Lovely. Just what you need, half the office knowing you've been dumped long before you do. You know all those dreadful things that chain letters threaten will happen if you break the chain? Well, they will be like a lovely long Caribbean holiday compared to what will befall you if you use the fax machine to give someone the kiss-off.

Post-it notes

Only the lowest of the low would do this to another human being.

Email

Acceptable only if the entire courtship has been a virtual one. Otherwise don't do it.

Text

See Email.

Some people think that breaking up over the telephone is unacceptable. I disagree. It all depends on how long you've been going with someone and how serious the relationship was. Obviously if you are leaving your husband and taking his kids, then a phone call is not how he should be informed.

Time & Place

Restaurants are a popular venue for the face-to-face break-up. Unfortunately this practice isn't in contravention of the Geneva Convention. It should be. Not only does a restaurant break-up ruin that particular eatery for ever more, there's the chance that you'll be put off your favourite dinner/dessert for the rest of eternity. Trust me you will always associate Chocolate Crème Brûlée with bad news in the future. No fair. No one should ever mess with a girl's favourite foods, most especially if it's Chocolate Crème Brûlée

Apart from all of that there's the humiliation factor. You really don't need every other diner in the place seeing you weep and jumping to the not-too-hard conclusion that a break-up is in progress. Unless you've signed up with a reality show, nobody deserves to have their humiliating moments shared by strangers.

Then there's the tried-and-tested tactic of pissing off the other person so much that they break it off with you. Boys just love this one. On paper it sounds perfectly reasonable but in reality it's cruel and horrible. One minute a girl is in a normal(ish) relationship and the next her BF is being consistently horrible and mean to her. It is far easier and quicker just to fess up and make a clean break.

> *Overnight Helen's seemingly nice and normal BF of a year,*
> *Robert, had turned into a monster. He kept cancelling dates at*
> *the last minute, didn't call when he said he would and got*
> *angry with her over the slightest thing. He began calling her late*
> *at night, long after her bedtime, and then got nasty with her*
> *when she wasn't able to talk to him. Two weeks went by during*
> *which the only contact Helen had with Robert was confined to*
> *their respective answering machines and the late-night calls*
> *where he would wake her up only to slam down the phone on*
> *her. Finally Helen had enough. She marched around to his flat*
> *and told him it was over. Helen later found out that he'd met*
> *someone else and had been too scared to let on.*

The worst break-up I ever experienced, in terms of sheer
meanness, was when I threw a party and my boyfriend
showed up – with *another girl*! This is NOT a good way to
announce the end of the relationship. Apart from that it was
very bad manners; the girl in question hadn't been invited.

> *Grainne felt honour-bound to end a relationship when the*
> *guy she was dating observed that all of their friends were*
> *settling down. "I think it's time to get the relationship thing*
> *sorted," he said. "Everybody else is moving in or getting married*
> *and you know, we get on well together and that, so I was*
> *thinking, you'll do."*
>
> *"Well, you won't," Grainne snapped and who can blame her?*

Never break it off in bed.

Bad Timing

Now obviously you shouldn't hang around in a relationship
that you don't want to be in. However, there are certain

times when you should just hold on for a bit longer. The following occasions are all officially *Bad Dump Days*:

His birthday, the week prior to and several days after. Come on, it's just not on, is it?

Valentine's Day and the preceding week.

Christmas, New Year's Eve and the week in between. Try it, and Santa will have you on the Naughty list for the next five years.

There are two exceptions to the above.

First Exception:

If your fella becomes physically and verbally abusive, dump him straight away. I don't care if his birthday falls on Christmas Day. Get out, the quicker the better, because it never gets any better.

Second Exception:

If you happen to discover that your BF is playing away and it's not too long till his birthday/Christmas/ Valentines. WAIT. Make sure there's a good crowd about before you give him his P45. Lastly, commiserate with him about his appendage. Feel free to use the phrase 'it's like a penis, only smaller'.

Now under normal circumstances I would lecture you about grudges and revenge-filled scenarios. I would tell you that they do more harm to you than they do the person who has provoked them. Yes, this is generally true. However a *Wandering Willy* has only himself to blame for his bad karma coming home to roost. In cases like this you are merely doing the

273

bidding of the universe and not being horribly petty. (Well, perhaps just a bit petty but under the circumstances . . .)

Never break it off on national television

We Need To Talk

The best possible way to break up is to meet the boy on neutral ground, somewhere discreet and quiet. Do not meet for a meal, instead have a coffee or a drink. Never break it off in the middle of a party or other public gathering. Unless he really really deserves it (see above). You introduce the subject by saying, *"We need to talk."*

That's it. Your work is basically done. Everyone in the English-speaking world knows that the combination of those four words signifies impending bad news. If your boyfriend says it, you know you are for the high jump. If your boss says it, you know that he's not going to be offering you a rise. If your best friend says it, expect some *Gerry Springer* style revelation to follow.

It's important that as soon as you utter the 'we need to talk' that you follow it up very quickly with the break-up speech. You cannot say 'we need to talk' and then head off for ten days on an Alaskan cruise. See, once the expression 'we need to talk' has been uttered it's all literally over, bar the shouting.

So you're in a neutral, discreet place where, and this is important, *the bill has already been taken care* of. Why? You need to be able to make a quick getaway if it all goes pear-shaped, that's why.

You say, "We need to talk," and he knows exactly what's coming. The hard part is over. However, you still need to deliver the actual bad news.

"I don't think we should see each other any more."

There, that's it. Done. OK, so he'll probably ask why and he's perfectly entitled to. So tell him. But be nice.

Standard Get Out Free Lines

We don't want the same things.
I'm just not ready for a commitment.
I'm a lesbian.

And the tried–and–trusted

It's not you, it's me!

A Field Guide to the Irish Male

The Civil Servant

How to Spot Him:

He looks absolutely nothing like a rugby player. In fact he looks as if he's never seen sunlight in his life. His grey pallor is matched by his grey suit and prematurely greying hair.

Habitat:

Leinster House, Powers Hotel, skiing holidays, Brussels and back rooms up and down the country

What he says:

"I have the Minister's ear."

What you'll never hear him say:

"The Minister was fully aware of the contents of the dossier."

PTBD: Post-traumatic Break-up Disorder

Chapter Twenty-nine

PTBD: Post-traumatic Break-up Disorder

Symptoms including but not limited to – boiling bunnies, drunken dialling and yo-yo sex

Whether you dumped or were dumped, the immediate aftermath is difficult. If you got your P45, then the chances are that you aren't exactly feeling great about yourself. This is fine in moderation. If you'd just been fired from a job you loved I wouldn't expect you to be jumping for joy. Take a bit of time for yourself – but don't isolate. An unoccupied mind has far too much time to re-run the relationship movie and drive you mad with the 'what ifs' and 'if only I hads'. There is no point in my telling you not to do this because we all do. Try to keep it to a minimum though. Get out and spend time with friends or get them to come around to your house and help you demolish the wine and crisps. This isn't just good for your head, it's good for your waistline.

It's OK to indulge yourself in misery but set limits. Give yourself time to give in to the misery but decide in advance when you are going to call it quits. Obviously the amount of time you spend mourning depends on the length and seriousness of the relationship that's just ended. There is the big difference between the end of a nineteen-year marriage and a six-monther.

When you do grieve, feel free to make an indent in the world's wine, chocolate and ice-cream supply (or crisps or whatever your vice is. I doubt it's carrot sticks and natural yogurt). Just go easy; the last thing you need when your self-esteem is in the crapper is for your clothing to start fitting a little bit too snugly.

When you are going through the post-break-up trauma, feel free to moan to your girlfriends. You'll know when to call a halt to it because you'll ultimately start to bore yourself. When that happens you'll know you're well on the road to recovery.

Sex With The Ex

Oh God, what can I say? Hands up who's done this. No, forget it. Hands up who hasn't. That will take less time. We've all done it, and usually it's not such a great idea. Post-break-up sex, like comedy, is all about timing. If you do have sex with the ex try not to do it until well after the break-up, in other words, until you are well over him. Otherwise, no matter how far you've come in the recovery process you'll be thrown right back to square one. The immediate aftermath will be a return to roaring crying in the bedroom, eating ice cream in the bath, and necking red wine straight from the bottle.

I know it's very tempting to jump back into the ex's arms at the first available opportunity but if you are even part way through the cry-fest, is it worth going through all of that again? Also, your friends who've been listening to you blab on and on about the demise of the relationship (as they are supposed to) will kill you.

What sometimes happens is a resumption of intimate relations can lead to a second go (or a third, or fourth) of the relationship. These yo-yo relationships are rarely successful. Try to remember that it ended for a reason and, no matter how good the sex, that reason will still be there in the morning.

> *Maggie was gutted when Paul, her boyfriend of two and a half years, broke it off with her. In the weeks following the break-up Maggie rang Paul a couple of times to see would he meet her for a drink. Each time Paul wouldn't, saying it was too soon. About a month after they split they met for a drink after which Paul drove Maggie home. Maggie was pure mortified about what happened next. She started roaring crying in the car and Paul, feeling guilty about how upset she was, accompanied her inside. "Then," Maggie said, "I can't believe what I did next – I begged him to stay the night. And if that wasn't bad enough, he refused."*

Maggie must have had a *really* sheltered life. I have yet to meet a girl who hasn't at some point in her life pleaded with her ex to spend the night. Yes, it's stupid, but you know what? We're all human and we all do silly things from time to time.

Given sufficient time and distance, sex with an ex need not be a pure disaster. If both of you are well and truly over each other and holding out no hope of a reunion then it can be worth the time and effort. In fact, ex-BFs can make pretty

281

good FBs, but only if all thoughts of a happy hand-in-hand walk into the sunset are behind both of you.

Break-Ups Without Cruelty

If you were the one getting your marching orders you had one of two reactions:

A. Relief.
B. Anger & Upset.

If you fall into the second category I don't expect you're feeling too pleased with yourself right now. Just remember not to take out your anger on innocent animals. In other words *Don't Boil His Bunny*.

Let Go.

Easier said than done at times I know. Been there, bought the white dress and curly blonde wig. Slipping into Bunnyboiler mode is a bad idea for the following reasons:

1. Why waste your time on a man who has no wish to go out with you? You are wasting valuable time when you could be out with other lovely boys who actually do value you.

2. You are in danger of having an injunction slapped upon you.

Now, we've all had our Bunnyboiler moments. Many years ago I was dumped in favour of another lassie. I have to admit I went a little bit crazy. One night I spent three hours on the

Internet and knowing only this woman's first name, which was rather unusual, and her profession, I found not only her last name but her address, telephone number and a picture of her. Why? Who knows? I was a woman quite literally obsessed. What was worse was when I saw her picture. Not only did I have a face to put on to the shadowy figure of my tortured imaginings but even more disturbing was the fact that it wasn't all that attractive a face. Talk about a final kick in the teeth!

I entertained fantasies of calling her up or arriving at her front door and letting her know just what a home-wrecking bitch she was. But, and here's the important part, I didn't. They remained fantasies and after a little while sanity returned from it's mini-break at the seaside and I got on with my life.

Then again, I don't drink and I shudder to think what I might have done with her address and telephone number if I'd downed a couple of gins. Getting langers when you break up with a lad is perfectly normal and acceptable behaviour. Just make sure you have someone to mind you when you're scuttered – someone who will stop you doing something that you'll regret later on. Something like calling him up.

Drunken Dialling

Don't Drink and Dial.

Just don't. You will always regret this in the morning – the bits you can remember. Drink and telephones just don't go together, ever. Have you ever been on the receiving end of a drunken phone call, or found a slurred monologue on your answering machine? Yes, well then you know just how cringe-making these calls are.

Now it's all well and good to have good intentions and make resolutions not to get jarred and call the ex. That's the problem with vast quantities of booze; the stupidest ideas seem brilliant. Late-night kebabs, spilling your secrets to near-strangers and calling the ex for a wee chat all seem inspired. They're not.

If you think you are in danger of drinking and dialling then take precautions.

1. Unhook the landline and lock the phone in a wardrobe or drawer. Then lock that wardrobe or drawer and lock that key away. Keep locking keys away until you run out of keys/places to lock. If you have to unlock several drawers in various locations throughout the house the chances are that you will:

   A. *Forget where the keys are hidden and/or what sequence they're hidden in.*

   B. *Get distracted by something else.*

   C. *Realise that calling the ex isn't such a good idea (unlikely).*

   D. *Pass out (quite likely).*

2. Give your mobile to your best friend to mind with instructions not to let you have it under any circumstances.

3. Make sure you have no change about your person to use in a public phone.

It goes without saying that you need to put all of these

safeguards in place before you hit the jar. It's a lot of work and I know that willingly abandoning your mobile will be like having a limb amputated but you will thank, and indeed still respect, yourself in the morning.

Old Whatshisname?

Getting over a failed relationship isn't easy. In fact it can be utter misery. When you're miserable it can be hard to believe you will ever be happy again. Just remember that everything passes – good stuff, bad stuff, tedious stuff, it all eventually goes away. The sun will eventually set on today and tomorrow, although you may not notice it, will be slightly better.

I had my heart broken once. Just the once I'm glad to say. It was one of the most miserable things I've ever endured in my life. I thought

I'd never meet anyone ever again.
I'd never want to be with anyone else ever again.
I'd never be happy ever again.
I'd never ever recover.

Nobody ever likes to admit to being wrong but on this occasion I'm delighted to tell you I was so incredibly, utterly and totally MISTAKEN! Talk about way off.

I did meet other men.
I did have incredible relationships.
I am happier now than I have ever been.

If you date someone and it doesn't work out, don't be too miserable about it. Remember the boy who you broke your heart in secondary school, or the one who dumped you in the middle of your college finals? Now what was that gom's name again? Wait now. It's on the tip of my tongue.

When things work it's great; when they don't it's an opportunity for something better. Remember that.

A Field Guide to the Irish Male

The Combover King

How to Spot Him:

CK is easy to spot – he has a few strands of hair carefully plastered over his bald pate. Some Combover Kings go in for elaborate weave-style variations on the basic comb over in an attempt to outwit the general populace. This doesn't work.

Habitat:

CK is happy anywhere as long as he's out of the wind and as far away as possible from electric fans, ceiling fans and helicopter blades.

What he says:

"Does this tub of Brylcream come in a larger size?"

What you'll never hear him say:

"Short back and sides, please."

Chapter Thirty

The End

Or is it only the beginning?

So there you are. You know the WHO, WHERE, WHEN and HOW. What happens afterwards is up to you. If you start a relationship with one of your dates then congratulations and best of luck for the future – and don't forget to invite me to the wedding.

So what if there isn't going to be a wedding? Well, then you just have to start all over again. That's not necessarily a bad thing. The most important thing about dating and/or searching for Mr. Right is that it's meant to be FUN.

The other thing you might start to notice is how jealous your married lady friends become when you're out several nights a week with different fellas. These days whenever I have a date I don't tell my married lady friends. Why? Because the following day I don't get a minute's peace as I'm constantly badgered with calls from the married mob looking for progress reports.

Married ladies are voracious. They want to know *everything*. No detail is too small for inclusion. What did he say? Where did you go? What was he wearing? What were you wearing? And on, and on, and on. Then when you've spent a precious half-hour during which you were actually supposed to be working, answering their every question they go all huffy if they don't like the answers.

"But I was dying to know what he was like in bed," they'll pout.

"Then you sleep with him," I'll say.

"Oh, for God's sake! Now you're just being stupid."

There has never been a better time for a girl to be single. Forget all of the Bridget Jones 'desperately looking for *the one*' nonsense. That was then, this is now, and things are very different indeed. We're still looking for the one but we're going to take our time and have fun doing it.

"It's not fair," the married ladies sigh. "I'm stuck home every night. Why do you get to go to all of these fancy places with all of these different men."

Because, you say, I'm SINGLE. I have no ties, no responsibilities and no commitments. Yes, it just isn't fair, is it?

Happy Dating & Enjoy Yourself,